James T. Quarles
1947

FUNDAMENTALS OF
CHORAL EXPRESSION

Hayes M. Fuhr

FUNDAMENTALS OF
CHORAL EXPRESSION

UNIVERSITY OF NEBRASKA PRESS
LINCOLN: 1944

To

THOSE YOUNG MEN AND WOMEN

WHOSE PARTICIPATION IN CHORAL ADVENTURE THROUGH THE YEARS

HAS STIMULATED THE FURTHER ADVENTURE

OF THIS BOOK

v

Contents

Foreword

UNDER the stimuli of public demand and a growing urge for artistic expression that would not be denied, the secondary schools of America have developed an over-all program of music education which certainly parallels most, and exceeds many, phases of mass education in the schools of our day.

The variety and scope of music activities, appreciation, and technical training offered to students of this generation are nothing short of remarkable, and form the basis of a valid hope that the cultural future of America will keep pace with its amazing growth in technology.

From the original basic premise that music study in secondary schools should be reserved for the few individuals who could be taught, in off hours, to sing or play together with tolerable efficiency, the concept of the place of music in the general education program has achieved parity with other great tenets in the creed of those who work for the adequate preparation of youth for constructive citizenship in a democracy.

A typical statement of the function of music education is that of James Mursell of Columbia Teachers College, who lists six major outcomes to be expected of the modern school music program:

1. A feeling for ideal values and for the uplifting power and message of beauty.
2. An independent and continuing interest, and so an agency for personal growth and self-fulfilment.
3. The tonic of a demanding and disciplinary experience.

4. Constructive and convincing experiences of a democratic type.
5. A means of recreation which can last throughout life.
6. The discovery of talent.[1]

Such breadth and scope of objectives substantiate the hope that every boy and girl in American schools will be given the opportunity to be warmed by the "divine fire," but they do not minimize the desirability or the necessity for specialized training for those who have the individual or group propensity for applied development. Rather do they increase the responsibility of leadership to supply the artistic challenge, guidance, and outlet which such comprehensive objectives engender.

It is both practical and essential that deep and constant research in provocative practices and procedures for developing specialized choral groups to their ultimate goals be made, and it is in commitment to this necessity that the current study has been developed.

It shall therefore be the author's aim in this work:

First, to condense the various fundamental problems which are inherent in all choral groups into five contiguous, interlocking units; second, to suggest means by which remedial or developing techniques may be applied in situations where they have not previously been employed, either through unfamiliarity with their efficacy or through retarded school or community background.

The five interlocking units are *group organization, repertoire, rehearsal, tone production, performance.* In the approach to the solution of these problems, there is no intent to imply that the formation and the function of choral groups represent primary objectives in second-

---

[1] James Mursell, *Music in American Schools*, Silver Burdette, Boston, 1943, pp. 13–28. (*By special permission of the publishers.*)

ary school music education. The contention is simply that: (1) specialized choral groups are a logical and stimulating outgrowth of an over-all program of fine art education; (2) they deserve discerning and capable leadership; (3) they should produce and can produce educational and musical experiences which constitute worthy components of education through music.

Consequently, it may be expected that the author will limit himself strictly to the technique of leadership and of performance in choral ensembles. The analysis and suggested treatment of the various problems are the result of unbiased study and investigation of procedures by leaders in the choral field whose achievements with both adolescent and adult groups have established standards of excellence which may be accepted as authoritative. A wholesome personal respect for the actuality of the problems is derived from thirty years of observation and combat with them.

FUNDAMENTALS OF
CHORAL EXPRESSION

CHAPTER ONE

Perspective

To be happy, to be satisfied, man must express himself in some way; and here in music, we have the ideal medium of expression. . . . It is only from things of the spirit that lasting satisfaction eventuates and among these music must be conceded to have a highly important place—possibly the most important. *

T HE realization of ultimate aims in the field of music lies in performance. Without sonant expression, the most exalted conceptions in this, one of the highest of art forms, are forced to lie sealed with other unused sources of power in the vaults of the great unknown. In literature, masses of readers may acquire kinship of appreciation without the texts ever being given oral expression; but while it is true that highly trained musicians may silently read music scores, hearing in imagination the progressions there set down, it is necessary to translate these written symbols into sound if adequate and complete expression is to be achieved. Since music is an art which requires a translating medium for consummation, it is essential that this medium have such technique, quality, and imagination as shall not only faithfully preserve the original conception, but add beauty and power thereto through the magic touch of applied expression. Without such an expression, the masterpieces of the ages are made impotent. With it the simplest folk songs may have power to sway multitudes. It is, therefore, incumbent upon those who deal with this element of expression that they have intelligent conceptions of the

* Peter W. Dykema and Karl E. Gehrkens, *High School Music,* Boston: C. C. Birchard, 1941, p. xxiv.

3

written symbols of creative music and that they develop a technique of performance which shall warrant its inclusion in the realm of art.

Conducting in both vocal and instrumental fields requires not only a comprehensive understanding of the score from the standpoint of mechanics, but also a knowledge of its meaning and implication. The conductor must intuitively sense the means that will best serve in performance to interpret the composer to the hearer; most of all, he must know how to develop the individual and communal abilities in his group, so that the performers may be able not only to master the technical requirements of the score, but also achieve that freedom and abandon in performance which satisfies the yearning for self-expression and uplifts and inspires those who listen.

VALUE OF SELF-EXPRESSION

The urge for self-expression is universal and transcends the boundaries of time, race, or environment. It is an inherent characteristic of man, and through the long history of humankind, since man first looked about him and realized that he was not alone, this urge has been manifesting itself in various ways throughout the life span of individual members of the species. Not all impulses for self-expression are desirable. Some are the vital concern of those who work for the progress of civilization. Not all are possible of realization, and the frustration of them creates complexes which strike deep into the vital processes of the individual, seriously affecting his reaction to his environment, his personal adjustment to society, and his ultimate achievement in life.

Singing, especially in groups, is an ideal medium for self-expression. Many individuals who have native capacity for singing are unable to free themselves sufficiently of personal inhibitions to express themselves adequately in solo performance. It is only in groups that restraint is overcome, and voice, mind, and soul combine to express not only the score, but, even more important, those nameless emotions and entities of the

4

spirit which, in their indulgence, leave the soul richer for its spending. There are multitudes whose talents, insufficient for individual performance, are yet adequate to make up the rank and file of choral units. For these, the experience of such activity is a priceless boon, since it gives to them individually— as members of the group—some little taste of the currents of exaltation which course through the souls of those more fortunate ones who have the means and the freedom of spirit to ascend the mountain tops of human expression alone.

UNIVERSALITY OF CHORAL PROBLEMS

Experience in adjudication and in choral conducting leads the mature director to the conviction that young conductors fail in the achievement of artistic results through the violation of—or the failure to employ—those fundamental principles which are applicable to all group performance. The frequent occurrence of the same violations with their undesirable results implies that if certain bad qualities of performance assume epidemic proportions in secondary school choral work, the more universal application of the relatively few fundamentals necessary for effective group singing would produce startling results which would likewise be epidemic in character—but of benign influence.

The further assertion is ventured that even in semi-rural communities and small schools, where the background, environment, and elementary training have been meager, praiseworthy and commendable results could be obtained if directors were more uniformly schooled in the application of these principles and had the patience and vision to put them into practice.

The most exalted performances of master units, steeped in choral tradition, are but elaborations and extensions of this simple technique, colored by the imagination of the conductor. Surely such kinship with the great and near great should be solace and encouragement for the pioneer director in outlying communities who must build new foundations, unaided by the past or by tradition. He may happily find that the discerning and undiscerning alike, who listen to his music, will realize that he has had contact with high places; they will be beneficially affected by the message of the music even if they do not wholly understand it. His supreme contribution, of course, will be the cumulative refining influences exerted upon those who reap the benefit of his training and idealism.

NECESSITY FOR ADEQUATE MUSICAL PREPARATION

Music has proved its right to inclusion in the most constructive and forward-looking curricula of the present day; and for the students, pride of craftsmanship and achievement should be concomitant with applied endeavor. To accomplish this, we must have able direction and a full acknowledgement of the place of music in the developing processes of the individual.

Many times tragedies are enacted in secondary schools under the guise of group performance. That the students and sometimes the directors do not realize the extent of the musical homicide does not make the situation less regrettable. The valiant but losing struggle of a group against obstacles erected through ignorance of cardinal principles of choral production is pitiful to witness. It sets up within the listener recurrent waves of inner rebellion that so wholesome and deserving a spirit of willingness and desire should reap such frustration. At such times one shudders at the sickening sense of defeat which must of necessity surge through the minds of the more sensitive singers who, through no fault of their own, are forced to collaborate in such musical degradation. The haunting fear arises that if such conditions are prolonged, the students may become indifferent, calloused to their applied mediocrity, and so be marred for life in the most sensitive areas of their being.

In such situations, it is not the spirit of music alone that is being violated, but more significantly the integrating processes

6

of the individual; for the ultimate good in all group music training lies not only in technically sound performance, but, as has been pointed out, in the freeing of emotional processes, which need expression for personal growth, and the fusing of individual efforts in common aim. Indifferent training can never accomplish these ends, and, when such group activities are forced into unskilled hands—be they ever so willing—the results are bound to be disintegrating and costly. Therefore, the institutions responsible for the training of teachers in the field must see to it that only those are encouraged to essay music leadership who have the rare qualities necessary for the task and that they be given so thorough a grounding in the fundamentals and ideals of the art that they may be able to open to youth new horizons of aesthetic adventure which are always waiting to be explored.

For the increasing number of supervisors in both large and small communities who are consistently turning out choral products that are a direct challenge to the most sophisticated, there is unqualified admiration. For those who are struggling along the upward way, earnestly striving to find the means to unlock the treasures of the musical wonder chest, aid is at hand in the sympathetic advice and counsel of those who themselves have been pilgrims on the toilsome road.

This book is an attempt to simplify and condense the fundamental necessities of choral procedure made traditional by leaders of vision and tested in the experiences of many years.

CHAPTER TWO

Group Organization

The function of the High School choral group is to give its members an experience that will enable them to grow in musical power and understanding, and to develop a deeper and wiser love for music as a fine art.*

IN outlining the fundamental elements of successful choral conducting, let us first consider the organization of the units which are to be developed. A thorough knowledge of the available individual resources is essential. Hence, the first objective of the supervisor should be a systematic vocal census of the high-school student body. At times, adverse psychology and sentiment against music activities are evident in schools, particularly among the male student population.

Individual auditions and friendly conferences can do much to break down these unnatural aversions which are usually the result of individual inferiority complexes, exaggerated self-consciousness, or a lack of stimulated interest. A frank personal approach, backed by sincerity and sympathetic understanding, can work wonders in setting up a psychology of willing co-operation and eagerness to try. If the enrollment is not too large for such a census, the consent of the administration should easily be gained for a complete per capita examination. This method serves to lend dignity and popularity to the music program and often results in the discovery of talent which, through reticence or lack of confidence in certain individuals, might not otherwise be found. In systems where the enrollment is too large for such examinations, the elective plan is

* Dykema and Gehrkens, *op. cit.,* p. 87.

employed, and auditions are given to those who apply. If the auditions fail to produce an adequate number of voices for the desired groups, the instructor may augment them through individual search for talent and through suggestions of other singers by those already enrolled. In either the elective or the total group examination plan, it is advisable to list names for audition appointments by alphabetical order or by classes, since determination of voice classification by the student himself is unwise and unsafe. For example, if a young woman thinks she is a soprano, and the director finds that the quality of her voice (which is the determining factor) points to mezzo-soprano or contralto, the "reduction in rank" may result in cyclonic repercussions from both the student and parents and may call for tact and diplomacy on the part of the supervisor in securing the student's cooperation and in making the correct classification without causing her a loss of "prestige." Such minor problems loom large in the music field at all times, but particularly so in the adolescent period. As is the case with many other distresses, prevention is the best cure.

PROCEDURE OF AUDITIONS

The individual auditions should be simple and not too long. Ten minutes is usually ample. An air of informality and naturalness should characterize all the examinations. The student should be put completely at ease and made to feel that the instructor has a definite, personal interest in his ability. Opportunities for highly efficient guidance are inherent in every interview, regardless of the musical outcome of the audition. Students who have solo material may be permitted to use it. Those who have not may be allowed to sing a number from a suggested list of simple folk or community songs, previously selected for the purpose and posted in the music room. *Quality, range,* and *intonation* of the voices are the chief elements to be noted. A transposition of the song, higher or lower, is a simple means of testing the range. Hence it is an invaluable asset to the director if he is able both to play the piano and

10

to transpose. Sopranos and tenors can thus be led to show extensions of range to upper *F* or *G,* and altos and basses from low *G* to upper *C* or *D.* To avoid forcing, an easy, soft tone should be encouraged. If the voice changes in the upper register, this should not be catalogued as a fault, since the change of quality may be only nature's rebuttal to strain in the middle voice. One should be alert for the discovery of light, free upper tones—no matter how soft—as they open the way to the promised land in choral singing.

CLASSIFICATION OF VOICES

It should be remembered that quality is the determining factor in voice classification. The heavier the natural quality, the lower is the classification. Exceptions to this rule are rare. That a girl with heavy, rich quality can sing to upper *F sharp* or *G* with full power does not necessarily mean that she is a soprano, for even though she may be able to execute occasional notes at that height, the tessitura of the voice may lie definitely in a lower range. If she is able to sing the upper notes only at a forte dynamic and with tension, the head voice is undeveloped, and she should be assigned to a lower classification until she learns how to produce the upper voice with ease. Straining for upper notes during the adolescent period is the greatest hazard in youth's singing and should be avoided at all costs.

Only those voices which can vocalize to the upper *F* and notes beyond in a light free tone should be classified as soprano or tenor. Any other classification induces objectionable choral quality and faulty intonation. Octave skips and scales sung downward on *oh* or *ah* with soft attacks on the upper notes are helpful in testing vocal resources and in orienting the singer in the proper classification. After the preliminary tests, the students assigned to alto, tenor, or bass sections may be asked to sing the appropriate part of a four-part song to show their reading ability. This procedure may not always be suc-

11

cessful inasmuch as many must be taught the foundations of part singing.

Students whose voices are in the process of change and whose ranges are inadequate for normal singing should be encouraged to wait until their voices are more secure. A list of these students should be kept, and periodic auditions should be given to test their development. Those whose pitch sense is definitely deficient should not be allowed to participate in specialized group singing. At times this practice may seem to verge on mental cruelty, but the resultant psychology occasioned by the use of chronically pitch-deficient singers is too hazardous to permit any other course of action. Tact and sympathy are essential in dealing with this problem, for many times these students are very eager to sing. In cases of arrested pitch sense, the teacher should suggest other avenues of self-expression which will prevent the development of a sense of inferiority, with its accompanying problems of social adjustment.

In small schools where tenors are bound to be in the minority, the supervisor should be on the alert to discover boy altos whose quality and range make an admirable substitute for mature tenors, and who may offer a happy solution to an otherwise baffling situation.

It is, of course, essential that yearly auditions for group personnel, both old and new, be scheduled. Classifications of former members of groups may need revision, since changes in the vocal mechanism occur with rapidity at the high-school age; in fact, the director should frequently check any voices which show tendencies of change.

An index of the results of each audition should be kept on appropriate forms, covering personal data of the student, his former experience and training if any, and pertinent notes on the voice—its quality, range, intonation, and maturity.[1] From

[1] For examples of convenient record form *cf.* Van A. Christy, *Glee Club and Chorus,* New York: G. Schirmer, 1940, p. 27; also Paul Van Bodegraven and Harry R. Wilson, *The School Music Conductor,* Chicago: Hall and McCreary, 1942, p. 55.

this index the instructor may proceed to the organization of the various units which are to function in the music program for the year.

ORGANIZATION OF UNITS

The medium school enrollment of one hundred to three hundred students should permit the development of boys' and girls' glee clubs and a mixed chorus, but care must be taken to achieve the correct balance of parts. It is much better to have a girls' or boys' glee club of sixteen to twenty-four members—all of whom can contribute their individual quota to the quality and accuracy of the group—than to include pitch-deficient voices which endanger the functioning of the ensemble and lower the morale. At times balanced performances by boys' and girls' groups numbering 12–16 voices may be found in clinics and festivals conducted by small schools. Though these are the exception rather than the rule, they are sufficient to prove that it is not in *size* but in *quality* that the secret of successful group singing lies.

The boys' and girls' units may be combined to study mixed voice literature, and additional singers may be permitted here, provided they have sufficient tonal accuracy and quality not to retard the progress and efficiency of the group.

The size of a girls' or boys' glee club or a mixed choir is usually dependent upon the available voice material in the *upper voice* sections. Occasionally other sectional material will be in the minority, but whatever it is, the part which has the *least number of useable voices must be the one around which the other sections are built.* Numerical proportions are not always a safe basis for determining the size of voice sections, for one or more mature voices in one may offset two or three in others. Usually the proportion of three sopranos, two second sopranos, and two altos, or multiples thereof, is workable in girls' groups. In boys' units the proportion of three first tenors, two second tenors, two baritones, and three basses ordinarily gives good results. However, remembering that a light free

13

tone is always to be employed in the upper voices, it may be that more can be used in the top sections than normal proportion admits. Or it may be that lower sections are so meager that they require an altered proportion.

In mixed groups it is usually practicable to use two to four sopranos for each tenor, with a normal ratio of three to two between sopranos and altos. The number of basses should usually slightly exceed that of the tenors in order to give solidarity to the chords. Good foundational bass is an admirable quality in all units in which men's voices are engaged. It should again be stressed that the whole matter of balance is not merely one of numerical proportion, but of the *tone core* of each section. Reference has been made to instances in which one or more mature voices in one section may offset a higher number in others. Just here lies an added difficulty, in that the "meaty" voice may, if indulged, stand out like an obbligato. It is patent that the good voices are the leaven of the choral bread, but they must not be as conspicious as raisins in the loaf! It is always safer, from the standpoint of diplomacy, to select the minimum number of useable voices for any unit refraining from a commitment that the selection represents the final quota, and then as the work proceeds, the director may add members to those sections which may need strengthening. This is much better procedure than to announce the total unit personnel and then be compelled either to make embarrassing adjustments later or to work with a group that is out of balance. It is wise to select a number of alternates. These may be summoned to replace members who may be lost through any cause or to add strength to a given part if needed.

UNACCOMPANIED GROUPS

As to the organization of strictly a cappella groups, two factors should be taken into consideration.

1. *The size of the student body.*—There are no arbitrary numerical limits for unaccompanied groups, but the a cappella idiom seems to function best in units numbering forty to

14

eighty members. Since membership in these organizations is highly selective, and since tenors, especially, are usually in the minority, it follows that this activity is most feasible in schools large enough to supply a requisite number of singers for each part. It is not a matter merely of learning to sing unaccompanied. It is a matter of balance.

2. *The effect of an a cappella group organization upon other possible choral units.*—If the development of such a choir results in the stress of that particular type of activity at the expense of the formation of less specialized units—for which there may exist less talented but none the less worthy student material—the balance should be thrown in the direction of more diverse and democratic types of activity with wider possibilities of participation.

There has been a tendency to make the existence of an a cappella choir the criterion by which the success of a musical activity program is judged. The result has been that some supervisors have used precious time, belonging to the school as a whole, in the attempt to keep up with musical "Joneses," whose enrollment, facilities, and membership material make that type of activity feasible.

Noble Cain says:

> In our zeal, many of us began to think that there was no music that was good unless it was a cappella. . . . This type of music constitutes the highest form of the choral art, but when we give all of our time and attention to the promotion of an a cappella choir, to the exclusion of other forms of choral singing, we are carrying it too far.[2]

There is no question that first quality unaccompanied singing represents a higher level of musical performance than does accompanied singing.

The technique of the capable a cappella choir entails a superior quality of pitch and interval consciousness—finer shading, nuance, and unanimity. However, it should be

[2] Noble Cain, "Choral Fads and Jitterbug Fancies," Music Educators National Conference, 1939.

remembered that a bad a cappella performance should not be condoned merely because it is a cappella. If, in young and inexperienced units, a choice must be made between singing off-key a cappella and singing on pitch with accompaniment, the decision should lie in the direction of the greatest accuracy. There are many secondary school organizations which specialize in strictly a cappella singing. They are highly commendable and have accomplished much for choral art; however, to eschew accompanied music is to narrow the horizon and rob the training period of much beautiful and effective song that includes an accompaniment as an integral part of the ensemble.

Secondary education should represent a general preparation for life rather than specialization in certain restricted fields, and it should be the business of the supervisor to open up to the student in the choral field the finest examples of literature of all types, thereby building a background which will help him to appreciate really fine music in the various idioms in which it is conceived.

THE GENERAL CHORUS AND SMALL ENSEMBLES

In order to give more general outlet for music expression than the above restricted groups permit, a general all-school chorus should be organized, for which there are no voice restrictions and to which all students are eligible. General chorus singing, when ably directed, can induce a mass musical experience which is highly provocative of aesthetic emotion and expression. For many such an experience can hardly be found in any other school activity. Hence participation in the general chorus should be unrestricted and the routine carefully planned to create and sustain interest.

The technique and musical literature of this type of activity do not logically come within the province of this work, but mention is made of the general chorus because of its great potentiality in stimulating and maintaining interest in group singing and in developing democratic musical comradeship in

16

the schools. Through the use of folk and community songs in unison or in parts, depending upon the resources of the group, a capable director can, without being too technical, achieve a mass expression of real beauty. Thereby he may not only be providing soul-filling experience for the rank and file but also an excellent background and stimulus for the more select groups which carry on.

Whenever possible, the formation of madrigal groups is strongly advised. They have a vocal idiom akin to the instrumental chamber ensemble and are definitely a cultural stimulus. Girls' and boys' small groups may likewise be feasible, but the supervisor should beware of "starting more than he can finish."

In general, then, the above are the suggestions offered for the procedure of group organization. Any routine must, perforce, be highly flexible, for each school has its inherent characteristics and problems with individual variations from the norm. Moreover, each new season will bring a change in the picture as far as the resources of talent are concerned.

The working plan of the supervisor should be so flexible that he can compensate for inadequacies in one field by excellencies in another, so emphasizing the latter that weaknesses are minimized and obscured and the results made to reveal the solid foundations of musicianship on which the work is built. Of such is the kingdom of musical art.

CHAPTER THREE

Repertoire

To ferret out compositions of sound musical worth is a great task. It is tedious and onerous labor; but in the process we shall find ourselves growing immeasurably; we shall find our knowledge widening and our understanding deepening, and we shall be producing programs fresh and stimulating to all concerned.*

THE quest for material for choral groups is like the quest for knowledge—it is never finished. Despite the fact that thousands of things have been written and are still being written for this purpose and that distributing agencies have catalogued and classified them with admirable completeness, it remains for the supervisor to make a personal research in this vast library to find material which will meet the many requirements his need may place upon it. The more meticulous and exacting he is in his standards of selection, the greater is the possibility of his being able to translate the written score into effective applied performance. Many a failure in the choral field is the direct result of poor choice of material, and many successes are largely due to the wise selection and use of repertoire. While it is not feasible here to discuss the multiple individual offerings of various publishers, there are certain general rules of procedure in the selection of material which, if followed, should guide the director into fields of research most likely to obtain desirable results. One thing is paramount: he should begin at the earliest possible moment to build a reference library of in-

---

* George Howerton, "Music Education Through Choral Experience," Music Educators National Conference, 1939.

dividual copies of numbers which have potential use in the various fields of his choral activity. Both personal and publishers' lists are valuable, but the careful accumulation of a comprehensive library of sources is indispensable to the progressive conductor.

GRADES OF DIFFICULTY IN REPERTOIRE

There is a very human tendency for directors to incline toward the use of material which is vocally too difficult for the secondary-school period. As proficiency in reading and musicianship develops, it is only natural that the conductor should look for new and more difficult worlds to conquer. However, it should be remembered that the voices in the high-school age do not develop maturity in the proportion that their minds learn to read and recognize intervals; and while the performance by high-school groups of music normally allotted to mature, adult voices may seem impressive, the strain put upon youthful voices in its rendition makes this a questionable procedure and potentially dangerous. It is not good technique to assign repertoire beyond the abilities of a group on the mistaken theory that mere difficulty of score automatically raises the level of performance. A strained and ineffectual rendition of a difficult piece, even if it be worthy, is no better than, if as good as, capable performance of a simple motet built largely on primary triads. "Better do easy music well, rather than difficult music poorly."[1] This does not mean that music of progressive difficulty should not be essayed. There must be growth and growth can be achieved only through progression from the simple to the complex. Care must be taken, however, that the material be kept within the vocal possibilities of the age group. If it demands more technique and reserve than are present, the rendition will be untrue to its tradition and hence ineffective. Added hazards will be loss of vocal quality through strain and inaccurate intonation, to both of which the student should be exposed as infrequently as possible.

When singers flounder about in repertoire which is too difficult, interest quickly wanes, and the whole function of the work is imperiled.

USE OF CHORAL ARRANGEMENTS

There is a growing tendency among publishers to offer arrangements of all kinds to the musical public, but the indiscriminate use of them is not to be encouraged. As in all other policies there are, of course, exceptions, and in order not to be unfair to vocal arrangements of all types, it should be said that some are less objectionable than others. The folk song type is acceptable, for the reason that the folk song was originally conceived to be sung by groups as well as by individuals, and the addition of choral harmonies is a natural elaboration which is consistent. Many talented composers have made settings of folk songs which preserve the integrity of the originals and which achieve a pure vocal idiom. But one must select with care, even from this field, for not all are equally successful.

When an arrangement draws upon the instrumental field for its original, the undesirable qualities are infinitely increased, for this type has not the virtue of possessing even a melody originally conceived for singing.

Choral directing is a difficult business at best and requires long and varied experience in order to achieve a maximum of musical and emotional expression. The least the young conductor can do is to adhere to the precept that choral music *originally written for the given ensemble is best.* From the vast store of all grades and types of material for vocal groups, let him choose repertoire which meets this standard. That will at least be a sound beginning.

Quite frequently, numbers written for one type of vocal ensemble are arranged for a different group. These are many times very successful and may be used when advisable. In the field of the classics, some very worthy musicians have lent their talent to the arrangement of classic ensemble literature for the various high-school units. These may be used with propriety and often with excellent results.

There are special occasions on which the use of choral arrangements is the logical answer to a need. However, the fact that they are more difficult to sing than pure ensemble music should restrict their use to a minimum, and limit the selection largely to those which retain, in the new setting, the *maximum vocal idiom*.

CRITERIA FOR REPERTOIRE SELECTION

What then should be the basic consideration in the selection of material?

As stated in the preceding chapter, it should be the conductor's business to open up representative choral literature of all types to his singers. Yet in choosing from this vast library, he should have certain basic qualifications in mind. Bodegraven and Wilson [3] list the following as essential characteristics of a highly functional repertoire:

1. It should fit the ability of each section of the ensemble.
2. It should hold the interest of the membership.
3. It should be conducive to finer technique and musical performance.
4. It should be educational as well as entertaining.

Another equally authoritative statement by Mursell and Glenn cites as requisites:[4] (1) Good melodic line; (2) interesting harmony; (3) wide range of dynamics; and (4) potential experience of beauty.

[3] Bodegraven and Wilson, *op. cit.*, p. 88.
[4] James L. Mursell and Mabelle Glenn, *Psychology of School Music Teaching*, New York: Silver Burdette, 1931, p. 282. (*By special permission of the publishers.*)

22

These two statements would seem to cover the essential qualities of repertoire, though there is still another element, perhaps implied in the above, which is increasingly looked upon as vital. It is the literary excellence and suitability of the text, certainly a positive need in any spiritual or educational objective.

Many splendid editions of early Italian, English, and German music have been published as the result of the sterling efforts of profound musicians who have a true vision of the choral field. Merely to ask for this type of material from the publishers specializing in it should bring immediate response in comprehensive approval consignments of examples that have a rich choral heritage and offer large dividends in development for the study involved. They are well within the capabilities of young groups and are in themselves conducive to finer musicianship and performance.

An interesting study of high-school students' interest in various types of choral music was made at an Illinois conference in which members of a massed festival chorus rated their preferences for ten compositions before and at the close of an intensive training period of four days. Out of a widely diverse list of styles, both sacred and secular, Palestrina's "Adoramus Te," one of the purest examples of the early Italian school, leaped from *last* to *second place* in the ballots. A modern Russian composition was first.[5]

POWER OF SACRED AND CLASSIC MUSIC

Much of the music suggested above is sacred in type, but this very fact commends it, since it voices a spiritual exaltation that is common to all creeds. In such repertoire may be found many examples which in color, emotional quality, and vocal style preserve the finest standards of choral art. Such material must be expected to emphasize pure vocalization, refined tone

[5] Max T. Krone and Florence M. Wallace, "High School Students' Interest in Choral Music," *Music Educators Journal*, Vol. XXI, No. 2, (Oct., 1934).

quality, beauty of phrasing, and sublimity of emotion, rather than mere tunefulness of melody and rhythmic patterns.

There is an innate power in classic music, such as envelops a master painting; and, in the practice and performance of it, students will experience the strange, new thrill that comes from the discovery of a type of expression which they have not previously experienced, and which stirs depths of aesthetic emotion that lighter types of music are powerless to sound. The effects of such study are both infectious and contagious and will result in the creation of individual and group taste in choral literature which will be cumulative and immeasurable for good. The use of such repertoire automatically provides membership in a musical fraternity whose standards prohibit indulgence in the commonplace. Units will be singing, not merely for amusement, but with spiritual and aesthetic aims which are created by the very nature of the music. No matter how isolated geographically such units may be, they will be maintaining traditions of culture which defy encroaching horizons and link them with the music aristocracy of the world.

CONTEMPORARY CHORAL MATERIAL

Another suggested type of commendable material is that of contemporary composers, which, again, is definitely written for the vocal ensemble. Many of these compositions are imaginative and have general acceptance among critics. Some have accompaniments, some are strictly a cappella, and some are optional. The same is characteristic of music in the classic field, though much of the latter is a cappella for the simple reason that it was written when instruments for accompanying were in process of development.

Choral music has a rich and powerful tradition. In developing choral groups as well as orchestras, it is wise to base the training on suitable classic forms which have stood the test of time and which are invaluable in preserving traditions of culture. We must not, however, worship exclusively at the shrine of tradition. Much modern music has proved its right to inclusion in the wide realms of art, and the variety, piquancy, and charm of many present-day offerings must not be overlooked or treated lightly. The forward-looking director will do well to include modern music in his unending research.

Finally, in selecting music for groups, one should beware of "best-sellers"—popular ditties and numbers designed to meet the so-called popular taste. It should be remembered that true music stirs the soul. It was not meant to agitate the feet!

> The way to keep good choral music as a daily fare is not to go to the other extreme and incorporate "swing" or popular material into the teaching routine. On the contrary, such music should be tolerated as amusement only. The permanent values remaining with students are rated, in after years, by the spiritual and cultural impressions made by *good music* and by a good teacher—never by a popular teacher with liberal fancies.[6]

Having set standards of type in his choice of material, the director must refuse to compromise. He should exercise care in scanning the voice line of compositions, being sure the voice range, particularly in the soprano and tenor, is within the possibilities of the group. He should concentrate on numbers that have a maximum of singing quality and sustained flowing style, that lend themselves to shading and subtle effects, and whose climaxes may be achieved *without loss of quality*. He should be individual and discriminating in taste, seeing the good in all that is worthy and avoiding the commonplace. So will he create a working library of material fitted to his need, a silent, vital force exerting a powerful influence in the building of all phases of choral enterprise. The results will impress themselves indelibly upon the student in his training period and will remain to ennoble the mature social processes of adult community life.

[6] Cain, "Choral Fads and Jitterbug Fancies," Music Educators National Conference, 1939.

CHAPTER FOUR

Rehearsal

⟫⟫⟨⟨

*For the singers as well as for
the conductor, . . . it is the rehearsal and not the concert that
most often spells adventure.*[*]

⟫⟫⟨⟨

JUST as "genius is the capacity for taking infinite pains," so
successful choral singing lies in the capacity for endless rehearsal. One spends years of daily concentration in the mastery
of an academic subject, and yet in such an intangible and abstract field as singing, the layman naively wonders at the
necessity for more than a few cursory rehearsals for any given
project in applied music activities.

Choral practice to the layman, and regrettably to some directors, consists in learning to sing the notes of any given piece.
If that were the aim, rehearsals might well be restricted, for
learning the notes is in itself comparatively simple. Learning
the notes is like a mountain climber crossing an Alpine
meadow beyond which lies the long, slow ascent to the tower-
ing summit.

The philosophy of labor saving in American industrial life
has unfortunately been reflected in the student approach to
many problems in which the capacity for taking time and infinite pains is a basic requirement. Nowhere is the philosophy
of "short-cuts" more fraught with evil result than in the realm
of music, for the application of such a philosophy to music
study moulds but a crude and lifeless effigy of the vital, living
spirit of the art. It must be remembered that in individual and
group singing we are building habits of reaction, first mental
and then physical. Moreover, in the physical reaction we must
train involuntary reflexes through the voluntary. This com-

* A. T. Davison, *Choral Conducting*, Cambridge: Harvard University
Press, 1940, p. 44.

plicated process must be employed in the breakdown of a wide variety of bad habits and the building of good ones through constant and long continued repetition of functional exercise under capable and patient direction.

HOUR AND FREQUENCY OF REHEARSAL

Athletic teams practice daily for extended periods during several months of the year, and no athlete is considered seasoned or dependable until his second or third year of training. Four years are employed in obtaining the basic knowledge of a language. Shall we consider that facility in music performance, either individual or collective, is less difficult of accomplishment than these? It is not in the province of this treatise to argue the relative importance of music with other activities and subject matter. It is pertinent, however, to point out that no more acceleration may be expected in music training than in other fields which demand mental and physical habit formation. Therefore, it should be the director's aim to hold rehearsals of specialized units as frequently as the circumstances and schedule will permit. They need not be long. In fact, short practices are preferable, inasmuch as limits of concentration and endurance are reached very quickly in this juvenile period of development. Daily practices of forty to fifty minutes are much more productive than prolonged biweekly or triweekly periods.

In the build-up of habit formation in the applied field it is the frequent repetition of correct routine for short intervals which makes for progress. Muscles are notoriously forgetful, and even professional artists, with established and grooved technique, must have daily practice. It is essential, therefore, in the juvenile stage of singing development, that there be a maximum of continuity in the habit-forming processes and a minimum of fallow periods in which to lose the mental and physical forms which provide the forward urge.

In many school systems there is no time provided in the daily program for choral rehearsal. This fact compels the units

28

to practice either before assembly in the morning or after the daily classes are over. Neither of these times is advantageous. Voices do not function at their best in the early morning. There is also a tension about such rehearsals that makes progress difficult. Whenever possible, it is far better for the choral activities if rehearsal can be worked into the late morning schedule, when the students are mentally and physically alert and when voices are at their physical best. If such a plan is impossible, late afternoon practices are more desirable than very early morning ones for the reason that voices relax during sleep and are slow to gain their natural muscular tone after rising. Range and pitch are very likely to cause difficulty in the early morning, and the discouraging results which often follow are due to a physiological factor which is beyond the director's control. Enthusiasm and willingness may, at least partially, overcome lethargy and fatigue in the after-school periods, but no amount of initiative or encouragement will compensate for the natural phenomenon of sleepy voices in the early morning.

REHEARSAL ENVIRONMENT

Surroundings have a very definite bearing upon the effectiveness of the rehearsal and should be regarded as important. Wherever possible, a room with raised tiers of seats is highly desirable. A gymnasium with bare, echoing walls is to be studiously avoided. The room should be well lighted, airy and comfortable; it should be of a type to lend itself to the intimacy of the choral program. It is desirable that the rehearsal room be devoted solely to music and that it develop the atmosphere of a place where art is studied and enjoyed. Let it be the "home" of the choral ensembles and, as such, let it be guarded and protected as is a real home from subversive or harmful influence.

Occasional rehearsal on the auditorium stage in the formal manner is desirable, provided the acoustics are favorable, but if the auditorium re-echoes when empty—as do some, unfortunately—like the echo gallery in the Mammoth Cave, the rehearsals in it should be held with stage curtains drawn or as rarely as necessities permit. One should never allow unfavorable physical surroundings which can be avoided to exact a penalty of even *one* unnatural or subnormal performance of a group. Good choral technique is an orchid of the musical hothouse and, as such, requires constant care and protection lest it wither and die.

Practice has proved that during the rehearsal period singing units function best when seated. After the repertoire is thoroughly learned, the group may stand for the rendition of individual numbers in order to grow accustomed to the performing position. In rehearsal, an erect sitting position with uncrossed feet should be insisted upon in order that the breath may function properly.

SEATING ARRANGEMENTS OF GROUPS

Definite seatings should be assigned with respect both to stature and to individual voices. Taller members as a rule should be at the center, provided the voice pattern will permit, for this arrangement makes the best appearance; but it is essential to place the singers so that the greatest homogeneity of quality and blend is secured. Therefore, the individual voice quality pattern must be the final determining factor. Pairing of voices within each section also helps to fuse individuals into group action.

Rows of members should not be too long. It is better to have four medium length rows than three long ones. Compactness is the aim, and no voices should be beyond the conductor's eye, either to right or to left. Widespread groups tend to break down a feeling of responsibility and of "belonging" for singers on the outer extremes of the ensemble. All details of seating should be very carefully planned to create a maximum of solidarity in the group, and each member should be made to feel his personal responsibility in the complete functioning of the whole.

In girls' and boys' groups the upper voices, traditionally, should be on the conductor's left, lower voices on his right. In mixed choirs there is more variation in seating, but the plan in which the tenors are behind the sopranos, and the basses to the rear of the altos is used by many choirs.

Some directors of mixed groups prefer to place tenors and basses in the center, flanked by sopranos on the right and altos on the left. The argument for this arrangement is that the boys' voices are thus concentrated and that their surety of intonation is thereby increased. Very few professional concert choirs use this plan, although in very large community or festival choirs it may be advisable to bank the male voices in the center to offset the power in the women's sections. By this method the director tries to secure equal balance between total male and female timbre.

Centering the male voices is also used as a means of disguising the relatively small number of boys' voices in one or the other of the two sections—usually the tenor—which would not only look ineffective but sound so against the larger numbers in the other sections. The shortage of manpower is often a real and baffling problem in small schools, and if a balanced four-part ensemble cannot be achieved through augmentation of a weak tenor section by boy or girl altos, it is better to use three-part music, as a four-part chorus with only suggestive tenor or bass is damaging to the objectives.

For public performance, the use of ramps is very definitely to be encouraged in all groups where two or more rows of singers are employed. The gain in compactness, unity, focus of attention, and tonal result is definite and conclusive.

THE ACCOMPANIMENT

The position of the piano and the accompanist is important. It must be remembered that an accompaniment, whenever used, is an integral part of the ensemble. In fact, it is probably the most important single element outside the direction.

FUNDAMENTALS OF CHORAL EXPRESSION

It seems hardly credible, but it is none the less a fact, that public performances may sometimes be heard in which the accompanist sits at the piano in a far removed portion of the stage with his back to the group and to the conductor. This is an exercise in telepathic synchronization which is both harrowing and fascinating to witness.

There are two logical positions for the piano. If it be a grand, it may be placed in the center front of the group with the keyboard to the left of the director as he faces the singers. Or it may be placed directly at the right of the sopranos and tenors at such an angle that the accompanist can see every movement of the conductor. This is a very practical position for an upright piano. If a grand is part of the equipment, the center position has the advantage of being in a location to be heard equally by all sections and easily to be fused into the ensemble.

The necessity of placing the instrument adjacent to a section that is subject to eruptions of colored intonation is the result of conditions which should never be allowed to reach the stage of discharge at the expense of the public.

CONDUCTING TECHNIQUE

As to the actual manual direction of group singing, there is a recent definite trend to the use of the hands rather than of the baton. The conspicuous success of many directors with ample baton technique, who have deliberately elected to use only the hands, is evidence that some very distinct advantages are inherent in that technique.

The complete visibility and exactness of the baton in the orchestral and opera fields and in large choruses, where the complexities of the score require meticulous guidance, is highly advantageous. There are, however, notable exceptions in which eminent conductors of symphonies and major choral groups have felt free to discard the baton and to use only the hands with highly satisfactory results.

In well-trained choral units, where intimate, sympathetic conceptions of rhythmic pattern, tempi, color, and dynamics have been built up through long and detailed rehearsal, the least of the functions of the director is to act as a metronomic governor. His much more exalted function is to paint tone pictures on a vocal canvas woven with the warp of correct rhythm and tempo and the woof of musicianly planned phrasing, diction, and dynamics. Subtlety and implication, high light and shadow should emerge through the deftness of his touch, and the means of their creation should be as inconspicuous as possible, lest the beauty of the picture be spoiled by the too obvious presence of the mechanics which call them into being.

Inspired choral conducting is that in which all technical elements of direction are submerged and in which the audience is conscious only of the fusion of the functions of both director and singers in the expression of exalted emotion. This concept of choral conducting does not imply that a thorough knowledge of the technique of the baton is nonessential. Quite to the contrary, it is imperative. Nothing is more pathetic than the aimless maneuvering of a director who merely makes motions in time with the music, so vague that even the practiced eye cannot discover the down beat, if any. Such manipulation is neither spirit nor body, and is no more effective in controlling the tonal product than a weather vane that swings at the whim of the passing breeze. The conductor must know the mechanics of his trade. All the varied patterns of execution for the various rhythms must be mastered and become automatic. Only then can he learn to relax the rigidity of complete formal outlines in his beat, and, retaining the necessary fundamentals of pattern, to add those synchronized motions which draw forth the subtleties of execution so necessary in vital choral expression.

Manuals of conducting technique are so common that it is not necessary to outline and discuss the beat patterns here. They should be studied and practiced until they become automatic and until the director is capable not only of performing

33

the appropriate movements for all rhythms, but of applying the correct patterns to the individual numbers in the repertoire.

In the early stages of choral conducting, the director usually experiences a keen embarrassment. He is unduly conscious of his hands and motions, which seem magnified into Gargantuan proportions. Only time and experience can relieve this self-consciousness. It is the result of lack of practice in coordinating mind and hands in rhythmic pattern, and it is not fatal. As in any physical exercise, grace of motion and form can be developed only with practice. The arm action should not be stiff and angular. Much of the motion should lie in the wrists, which must be supple and sensitive. Large motions are not essential. In fact, the more the area of action is reduced and concentrated, the more intense will be the attention of the group. Just as we naturally concentrate closely in looking at small objects, so does the director, by limiting and intensifying his field of motion, compel minute concentration on the part of those who look to him for guidance. Since every sound that issues from each individual should be under the direct control of the conductor's hands, it stands to reason that concentration can not be too great.

Women ordinarily find more difficulty in developing freedom and confidence in conducting than do men. This may be but a natural timidity of the sex, but there is no reason why they may not be highly effective conductors of choral singing, granted that their background, training, and practice are sufficient. In fact, their inherent grace and refinement of motion should be an asset.

At times the sense of personal embarrassment in conducting is so keen that groups are allowed to sing without direction. This is hazardous and can never be successful. None but the small ensembles should be allowed public performance without guidance.

To summarize the technique of the use of the baton or hands, then, the director should be supreme in the control of his group at all times. His manner should be direct and forceful but only sufficiently demonstrative to obtain desired results from the unit. He is not directing the audience but the singers, and all his movements should be aimed at this single objective. Timid, self-conscious directing inhibits the action of the ensemble which must depend upon the conductor for guidance on every tone. On the other hand, wasted, elaborate motion worries the listener, confuses the singers, and endangers unity. Attacks and phrase endings must be definite; shadings must be indicated; and the tempo and rhythm must always be under complete control. With such a technique covering all phases of performance, the groups will soon learn to recognize instantly the desires of the conductor and to translate them into vocal action. When this stage is reached, "concerts may well be no more than exciting interruptions of the process by which the powers of the chorus are developed," [1] and occasions of even greater thrill for the singers and the director than for the audience.

THE REHEARSAL ROUTINE

As to the routine of the rehearsal period, there is no infallible recipe for success, but there are a few beacons which light the way to growth and progress.

First, there is the matter of attendance. No choral group ever achieves significance whose membership is not willing to fight for it. Fortunately, like a democracy, group singing has some things worth fighting for. Regular attendance is simply indispensable and that is that! In this "day of grace" and activities the battle against time is relentless, but some things are going to win. Why not music? Iron discipline is not the ultimate answer to attendance. There are only two: the music and the quality of direction. If both are inspiring, the problem is solved; if only one, the prognosis is not favorable; if neither, there is no need for an autopsy.

[1] A. T. Davison, *Choral Conducting*, Cambridge: Harvard University Press, 1940, p. 43.

Second, there is the matter of attention. This term connotes respect, and the ability to command respect is a sublime attribute in a conductor. Mere camaraderie will not attain it. Aloofness, indifference to the personnel and to the music, or an "All Passion Spent" attitude will never command it; rather the *love* of the *music,* patience, a goal, and a certain intangible but definite boundary between director and student will forever foster its growth. The latter is one of the most subtle and powerful factors in teacher-student relationship. The director must be a very human person—easy to approach, vitally interested in his students as *personalities,* and possessed of a ready sense of humor; but with it all, a certain dignity must sit upon him which epitomizes the art he serves and which no informality nor comradeship of effort should ever quite dispel.

Again, there is the matter of variety. Rehearsals should be so well planned in advance that they will create and sustain interest. Prolonged practice on one piece or on one style of composition should be avoided. Various numbers of the repertoire should have a hearing, diverse types being alternated. This mode of procedure keeps singers on their mettle and stresses contrasting elements of performance. Let the first number to be rehearsed be a favorite, or be of a type to incite immediate interest. There should be occasional short periods of relaxation, during which there may be as much freedom as the director feels is justified. These are good moments for short informal chats with individual chorus members or with sections, which humanize the project and beget cooperation. One should not attempt to cover too much ground at any one rehearsal. It is better to make a limited number of details secure and then to let them season until the next practice. *Every rehearsal should give the individual singers a sense of something well done.* Whatever that something is, let the director commend it heartily. Too much criticism leads singers to feel that nothing they may do is correct. An able physician does not tell a sick patient all the details of his ailment; neither should the director tell the chorus all that is faulty with its technique. He should be satisfied with slow but steady progress in the elimination of faults.

Last, there is the matter of the conductor's familiarity with the music he directs. Does anyone doubt that one of the commanding attributes of Arturo Toscanini's art is his complete memorization of all the music he conducts? Let the director make it his aim to know every part and parcel of his music and find truly that Knowledge is Power.

Given a happy fusion of interests in a field of art expression that is as varied as the hues of an autumn sunset, the conductor and his singers, out of a background of thorough knowledge of the music, and a mutual understanding of and respect for one another, will be collaborating in imaginative enterprise that transcends all mechanics and leaves them free to roam the realms of musical fancy.

CHAPTER FIVE

Tone Production

>>>-<<<

*Tone is an intoxicant which needs
the most careful consideration. Rightly
utilized, it affords a marvelous outlet
for a healthy emotional urge. Sometimes I have thought that the greatest
curse as well as the greatest blessing of
music as we know it is its very essence
—tone.**

>>>-<<<

IN tone quality we have one of the greatest potentialities for
good or ill in all the field of music. Since musical performance
in its final analysis is but extended and elaborated tone, it is
patent that the finer the quality, the more effective will be the
result. On the basic fundamental of good tone quality must, of
course, be built a superstructure of technical facility; but no
matter how great the skill in other phases of performance, if
there is not the basic quality of inherently beautiful tone, the
result will be commonplace.

Through some whim of the muse who directs the fate of
those who strive for musical expression, it is possible to attain
a rather elaborate technique and facility without beauty of
quality. One might wish that there could be a natural barrier
beyond which the singer or instrumentalist might not go until
he has achieved this fundamental. Tone quality is like the
element of love in the thirteenth chapter of 1st Corinthians,
which, adapted to singing, might read: Though I sing with the
tongues of men in many languages, and have not good tone
quality, I am become as sounding brass or tinkling cymbal. And
though I have the gift of talent and understand all music and
all tradition, and though I have all technique so that I can
astound multitudes, and have not good tone quality, I am

* J. L. Lansbury, "Education Through Music," Music Educators National Conference, 1939.

nothing. . . . And now abideth technique, interpretation, and tone quality, these three, but the greatest of these is tone quality.

There is an innate appeal in beautiful tone which instantly registers itself upon the ear of both the layman and the schooled musician. Brilliance of technique may excite awe and admiration, but unless it voices a succession of appealing tones, even the uninitiated will realize that something is amiss. When beautiful tone quality is present, even repertoire above the level of the hearer's comprehension becomes impressive; and when it voices music which is on the plane of his appreciation, a thrill of response is quickened which lingers to sweeten the memory, sometimes for years. Mabelle Glenn has said, "When beautiful tone is used as the instrument through which a worthy thought is expressed, the audience does not walk out, no matter how untrained it is in music. It may be untrained, but not unconscious of emotional appeal." [1]

What do the people who heard Jenny Lind or Adeline Patti remember—the scintillating brilliance of their execution, or the poignant, golden notes which poured forth in some Swedish folk song or in "Home Sweet Home"? Had their voices lacked the luscious quality which was theirs, even the simple ballads of the people would have been ineffective, but through the priceless medium of haunting quality, the memory of those unforgettable moments remains untarnished by the years.

Beautiful tone is an indispensable element, therefore, in all types of music performance and *"the primary requisite for choral effectiveness."* [2] No amount of superiority in other elements of rendition can atone for its absence. In singing, beauty of tone transcends even the text and is eloquent in any language or in none, for it voices itself in a medium which emotionally stirs singers and audience alike.

[1] Mabelle Glenn, "A New Goal in Ensemble Singing," *Music Educators Journal*, Vol. XV, No. 1 (October, 1928).

[2] Wm. J. Finn, *The Art of the Choral Conductor*, Boston: C. C. Birchard, 1941, p. 3.

STRUCTURE OF THE GROUP TONE

There is a certain paradox existent in group singing which is an encouraging element in unit development. It is that the group tone product can be made to excell that of the individual members who comprise the personnel. Archibald T. Davison refers to this phenomenon as "distinguished mediocrity" [3] in the sense that the separate voices are often mediocre and assume distinction only when merged into homogeneity under capable direction.

In the massing of voices, either the worst or the best qualities may be magnified. If bad qualities are allowed indulgence, the result will be merely exaggerated error; if the best that each has to offer is encouraged, the objectionable individual elements will be attenuated and the good augmented. In this salutary phenomenon of fusion lies the cue to the means by which a schooled director can achieve remarkable results from raw material which, at its individual best, is but mediocre.

However, the better the individual voices are by nature, or may be made through training, the finer will be the group tonal result. Even though the efforts of the individual must be submerged in those of the group, the director must understand the physical properties of individual voice production and be able to apply them to the ensemble.

CHARACTERISTICS OF THE INDIVIDUAL VOICE

The singer's individual voice quality is a part of his natural endowment. It is as inherent as personality, and no amount of training can create it if the original capacity and endowment are lacking. However, like personality, which many times is submerged or stunted, whatever capacity is existent can be developed. Almost every normal person can sing, but the degree of excellence which he can attain is determined by the amount of his initial gift, his interest in the art, and his emotional reactions to certain stimuli.

[3] Davison, *op. cit.*, p. 59.

Again, tone quality has varying degrees of appeal in different singers, depending upon natural forces inherent in the individual. Thousands of violins give back pleasing tone when played by capable performers, but it remained for Stradivarius to achieve the heights of human accomplishment in violin making. Why? Not because of the capacity of his instruments for more extended technical brilliance, but because of a quality of tone which the consecrated hands of their creator were able to enclose within the wooden framework. Accordingly, thousands of voices may in varying degrees be pleasing and attractive; but only a few individuals have been so touched by their Creator that, through intangible media which no man may fathom, they sing with a quality which enshrines them in the memory of their own and succeeding generations.

In discussing the factors necessary for the production of superior singing tone, it is essential first to point out certain physical properties of agreeable sound, and then to suggest means of its development by the individual, for the success of any choral adventure is determined by the capacity of the individual participants to contribute their personal quota to the whole.

The character and quality of tone are dependent upon three factors: namely, the nature of the vibrating medium, the structure of its resonator, and the ratio of its overtones to the fundamental. In the human voice the vibrating medium is the vocal bands which are set in vibration through the impulse of the breath. Phonation is accomplished through coordination of ear, mind, and larynx, by which the vocal chords are made to respond with the correct number of vibrations necessary to produce the required pitch. It is one of the natural wonders of this fascinating mechanism that these slim chords or bands in the larynx can, through the coordination of ear, mind, and larynx, execute the correct number of vibrations per second to produce instantaneously single tones or scales of great rapidity. After the waves of vibration are set in motion, they are reinforced through resonation which may be felt in three localities,

42

according to the relative pitch of the tone. In low notes the concentration of resonance is more in the chest; in middle tones it is felt strongly in the roof of the mouth; in upper notes the sensation is felt in the head and in the facial cavities behind the nose. Hard structures give back more reinforcement of tone than do porous or yielding ones, and thus nature has endowed man with bony cavities, against which the speaking and singing voice may resound and be reinforced. The degree of freedom which the voice has in access to these resonators determines to a very large degree the vitality and effectiveness of the singing tone.

CONFLICTING THEORIES OF VOICE PRODUCTION

Everyone who sings is thoroughly familiar with the sensation of changes in his voice, and the more unschooled the singer, the more apparent are these changes. In singing upward, the amateur finds sooner or later, and usually sooner, that the strain is increased with each ascending note until he arrives at a pitch beyond which he cannot ascend without so changing the production and quality that the ensuing tones seem completely foreign to his normal voice.

Since the acquisition of range is progressively vital in singing efficiency, it is but natural that learning to produce high tones with ease should have been the most coveted goal in singing since man learned to express himself through the medium of song.

Controversies which have arisen around the extension of the voice upward have characterized each succeeding vocal generation and have been both heated and prolonged. So-called "methods of tone production" have been evolved by the score, following the principles of "maestri" who have been conspicuously successful, or singers who have been blessed by nature with mechanisms which enabled them to sing without difficulty, and who have set about teaching others, less fortunate, the secrets of attaining this coveted aim. All the various parts of the vocal organism have been utilized as key factors

43

in these multitudinous approaches to technique; and the "thousand natural ills" to which the voice is heir have been diagnosed and prescribed for in the light of violations of precepts governing the physical action of the "pet areas."

Thus we have many divergent schools of vocal theory. There are those who hold that the breath is the "summum bonum" of the art; those who stress a low or a high larynx during the singing act; the disciples of the crisp attack, attained through vital action of the vocal chords at the start of the tone; the resonance school which solves all problems by singing on a given timbre; those who preach forward placement on the lips and in the masque as the true aim; those who hold that registers are a natural series of compartmental adjustments arranged for our aid, as well as their opponents who say that registers are purely the effect of bad singing; the conservatives who declare that each tone is a register in itself; and finally the school which treats the whole singing problem as mental rather than physical and holds that singing is merely the phonation of a mental concept which, if it be correct, needs only freedom from bodily tension to function successfully.

In such a welter of currents and crosscurrents, beliefs and disbeliefs, what is the poor student or striving director to believe? Are there any points of agreement in all these views? Happily there are. Although all do not have the same recipe for tone production, all agree that resonance or intensity or ring, whatever it is called, is concomitant with good tone. Why, then, are there so many differences of approach? If the human voice had a compass of only a comparatively few notes, there would probably be very few different "methods" of tone production. It is the extension of range that causes most of the difficulty, and since the necessity for commendable quality and color of tone is generally accepted as the primary goal, the wide differentiation in methods of teaching is mainly due to quest for range without impairment of quality and without increased tension. Methods of production finally stand or fall by the degree of success they attain in bringing an extended scale into the use and control of the singer.

Not only have controversies arisen among exponents of individual methods of approach to this baffling problem, but scientists, in order to solve the mysteries which lie hidden in the human larynx, have entered the field with modern mechanisms for measurement of acoustical properties of the voice and for photographing the vocal chords in action. Physicians and throat specialists have attempted to formulate principles of tone production and methods of training on the basis of physiological data. All of this research and variety of approach have resulted in a more universal interest in the art and have stimulated vast numbers to attempt to sing, but it remains for the chosen few in any generation—those few who have been endowed by nature not only with the capacity for both quality and range, but also with the rare personality and temperament necessary to exploit them—to rise above the common level.

THE FACTOR OF INDIVIDUAL ENDOWMENT

Thousands of people swim or play golf or tennis passably well. Indeed, at certain times for brief periods their technique may be wholly correct. Why must they then forever remain in the field of the capable amateur? Is it the lack of practice or of a sound technique? Perhaps these are contributing factors in their failure to do better than they do, but the unalterable fact remains that, practice and technique notwithstanding, there is a lack of certain intangible elements in the inherent capacity of the individual, certain failures of coordination, or inferiorities of organic structure—all of which ultimately prevent him from attaining mastery in those fields.

Singing is a perfect parallel to this example; in singing, however, we have an even more intangible factor in the emotional element, and so virtuosity is more rare. Realizing the infrequency of profound initial capacity, should we be deterred from attempting to sing, either individually or collectively? Certainly not! The proportion of creditable performances is certainly as great in this field as in others which produce varying degrees of proficiency. We simply must recognize the invincibility of the natural laws of limitation in individual endowment and, to use a homely expression, forbear from the futility of trying to build telegraph poles out of fence posts. Need it be added that both have their uses?

It is not in the province of this work to project the training routine for individual vocal development. The training of a soloist is a highly specialized process in which methods of approach must be adapted to the particular needs of each student. There are, none the less, certain fundamental principles of individual tone production which are applicable to group singing and which may be applied with resultant good to the mass production. With these we now shall deal

BREATHING

Man has a pair of bellows which must inflate and empty in regular pulsation if he is either to speak, to sing, or to exist. In normal living, awake or asleep, we carry on this function automatically and unconsciously, and it is only when we have need of more air fuel for exercise or prolonged vocal action that we become aware of the necessity to increase and conserve it.

All the breath which we inhale goes in and out through the vocal chords. So long as we are mute, the chords remain unflexed and disengaged, offering no resistance to the entrance or outgo of the breath. When we speak or sing, however, the chords tense themselves, approximate, and offer resistance to the breath. This act of resistance puts the breath under pressure, which reacts again upon the vocal bands, causing them to vibrate and so to create sound.

Ordinary speech is constantly interrupted by staccato-like pauses in which we unconsciously renew the loss of breath supply; we can instantaneously raise the voice, cry out, or sing a note without any sense of breathlessness, merely because the bounty of nature gives us sufficient reserves for such action.

When we sing, however, we extend the vocal sound without interruption for some seconds, and thus our normal reserve is insufficient for the added requirement. This does not necessarily mean that much more air is actually expended in the singing process, for, remember, the chords are resisting the outgo of the breath. Rather it means that there must be sufficient air in the lungs, under pressure, to keep the chords resistant for the duration of the note or phrase. Herein lies the crux of the whole matter: we must have enough air under pressure to keep the vocal bands sufficiently resistant to create the tone vibrations; and we must adjust the air volume and pressure so that we sing with the same ease and unconsciousness with which we speak.

Fortunately, this finely adjusted and somewhat intricate process requires little of the singer but willingness to try, for nature has so marvelously adapted the component parts of our breathing apparatus to their function that if we insist on naturalness in our approach to the problem, the breath apparatus will automatically take care of itself.

Thus automatically we learn to take the right amount of breath, not by inflating our chests to the bursting point, but by quietly allowing our lungs to fill deeply and satisfyingly as though in vast content. Lung expansion is not in one direction, be it remembered. If we try to breathe exclusively in one place, we reap tension in that area. Nature permits us to hold the chest erect with comfort so that it will not compress the lungs—unless, through careless habits of posture, we have acquired a flat chest and slumped shoulders; she has detached the lower ribs from the sternum so they may expand easily in front and back, and she has supplied us with a flexible membrane in the diaphragm, which alternately draws in and propels the breath from the body. Chest, ribs, and diaphragm combined have the capacity to enlarge the area of the expanding lungs, and likewise the capacity to retain and to exert pressure upon the air after it is taken.

Hence, if one should place his hands upon a singer's midriff or on his dorsal ribs, or yet on his lower back, he should feel expansion when the breath is inhaled; but if he should lay his hands upon the singer's chest or shoulders, he should find them motionless, for chest and clavicular breathing is the breath of exhaustion, and of that there should be none in singing.

Father William J. Finn very aptly epitomizes the act of breathing for singing thus: "Keep the shoulders down and breathe as deeply as possible." [4] By this the eminent conductor does not mean that the depth of breathing should be concentrated in any one direction or area. Abdominal breathing is as radical and extreme as the clavicular type. On inhalation, a normal expansion is felt in the area below the sternum, but this does not mean that the further and deeper one protudes the abdomen, the fuller is his breath. We cannot, after all, breathe other than with the lungs; and since the diaphragm is the division wall between the lungs and the digestive tract, it must also constitute the boundary of expansive action in that direction. To manipulate the lower abdomen in breathing is to substitute artificial muscular motion for lung expansion and to subject the digestive mechanism to indignities which it resents.

As a matter of fact, the lower abdomen should be rather firmly compressed in order to give poise and erectness to the chest and to maintain muscular tone in the abdominal wall. Deep breathing therefore is largely a matter of poise of the body, which, if correct, allows the diaphragm, ribs, and back to coordinate in providing room for a developing, easy lung expansion, which is indispensable for singing and a vital element in well-being.

TONE PRODUCTION

In the adolescent period we have a physically immature stage of voice development which has certain definite characteristics,

[4] Finn, *op. cit.*, p. 25.

and which creates very well-defined boundaries within which the voices must be kept if singing is to be effective and unharmful.

At this age the vocal organisms of both girls and boys enter the sphere of development which gradually brings maturity. Until this time the voices have been child organisms with child reactions. The boys' voices, of course, go through a pronounced change and assume characteristics, but not full possession, of adult male production. At this age the vocal chords have not the tendinous vitality of the adult, and the thoracic, diaphragmatic, and abdominal muscles are likewise limited in development. Thus it is entirely reasonable to expect that the voices, whatever their mature type is to be, will function easily only through a type of production which puts no undue strain upon youthful mechanism, nor demands more of the organs involved than they are physiologically able to produce. In this simple and common-sense conception of voices at this stage lies the whole secret of approach to adolescent group singing activity.

In this period there is an inherent charm about the quality of voices when protected from strain, which is quite unique; one wonders that through misguided objectives it should ever be violated.

Noble Cain says that the adolescent voices of high-school age, when controlled, are "so beautiful that all the color and warmth of tropical islands seem to emanate from them." [5] This type of vocalism, however, is as yet the exception rather than the rule; the unmusical sounds which characterize many of the ensembles in our schools prove that there are still few supervisors who realize that "ensemble singing is a precise specialty and that the feats of concerted ventriloquism which for so long have passed as choral singing, are an affront to the art." [6]

[5] Noble Cain, *Choral Music and Its Practice*, New York: Witmark & Sons, 1932, p. 7.

[6] Finn, *op. cit.*, p. 11.

It can be expected that individual dramatic voice quality will be found but rarely at this age; and that when found, the range of notes on which it can be used will be small. This is not, however, the type of group voice quality that we are seeking, and so the comparative rarity of the vibrant solo type of voice need not dismay us.

GIRLS' VOICES

In the search for a tone quality that may be made homogeneous, we turn first to the girls' voices, for the director must know how to train the voices of the individual sections of his unit scientifically and how to merge all parts into a homogeneous blend.

Girls' voices at the adolescent age characteristically have a light, almost ethereal, fluty quality and though the range extension may not be great, many sopranos will be found who can comfortably sing to *G* or *A flat* above the staff in this manner. The scale pattern will run more or less true to form. In singing upward, usually a firm tone will be used to *C* or *D* middle staff. Here the voice will change quality and a lighter tone will emerge. In certain individuals the heavier quality will extend itself to *E flat* or *F* upper staff. But wherever the change occurs, the students should be encouraged to concentrate on the light upper quality and, through practice, to extend it downward. Under no circumstances should the heavier tone be forced upward to the point where tension and loss of quality are incurred.

That the upper tone will be small and sometimes veiled may be expected, but that fact should constitute no deterrent to its use. Once having established the tone, it may be extended upward as far as perfect freedom will permit, and it should certainly be carried downward as far into the middle tones as possible. It may be well to clarify the student's concept of the quality by frankly calling it "head tone" which, once it is established as a pattern, should be practiced diligently. It will be found that if quiet, deep breathing is encouraged and no premium is put upon volume—only upon ease—the voice will begin to extend itself upward; this is the aim to be sought. At the same time, the systematic downward extension of this quality will tend to smooth out the roughness and inequality of the middle range. Moreover, the routine use of the light quality will strengthen the mechanism of the upper voice and the ability to crescendo without change in tone quality will gradually be acquired.

For individual or group vocalization the use of slow down-scale exercises will be found helpful in establishing the tone pattern and in carrying it downward as well as in extending it upward. The breath must be deep and quiet, the attack gentle and clear, and the tone of soft, floating quality, with no changes or adulterations as the pitch descends. There should be no effort in the throat. The scales should be sung slowly and softly on *oo, oh,* and *ee*—later, with *ah.* Breath may be taken at each alternate tone. The *ee* should have an *oo* color—like the German umlaut or the French *u* with the lips slightly pursed. The exercises may start at *E flat,* top space, continuing downward to *C* and upward as far as ease of production permits.

Any other simple, melodious, down-scale exercises may be used until the sopranos lose all consciousness or fear of the upper range, but be it understood that vocalises are not the only medium for achieving the tone. Actual song literature, practiced at first on *oo, oh,* or *ee,* is sound procedure. One should never tire the singers with mere vocalization. The essential thing is to implant firmly in their minds the "tone pattern"—to give them the concept, first, of the sensation of absolute freedom in tone emission, and, second, of a quality that seems to *float on the breath.* If pianissimo is insisted upon, the element of freedom will first be established; then the tone will begin to gather intensity through unhampered contact with the resonators, and crescendos will emerge as a natural consequence. 17383

The same general procedure should be used for mezzo-sopranos and altos except that in these voices a heavy chest quality may exist from the lowest tones up to *E* or *F*, bottom staff. The break in these voices at that point or higher, if the voice has been incorrectly used, is likely to be both abrupt and radical; for the alto uses a quality in the deep tones akin to the male voice, and the transition from this tone to the typically female one is pronounced. The heavier the chest quality, the more radical will be the change. It is vitally essential that the use of the chest tones be kept to those notes below *E*, first line staff, as any extension of the quality upward puts a severe strain upon the mechanism and weakens the adjacent light tones. Similar exercises to the ones used for soprano are excellent routine and will help to build a structure of upper notes which otherwise may be impossible of acquisition. The exercises may start at *C*, third space. Closed vowels should be stressed, and the chest quality should be allowed to enter on down scales only after the danger area adjacent to the *E* natural is passed. Such exercises help to establish in the alto section a lyric quality which is capable of fascinating effect and which forms an admirable foil for the soprano.

If group exercises are used, they may start with the altos, the various sections dropping out or joining in at the logical intervals for each section. In this type of technique it will be stimulating to find that ordinary range limits disappear.

The menace of "topless" voices with their attributes of strained quality, flattened pitch, and utter incapacity to sing sustained phrases should quicken directors to make use of this simple but very sound procedure. The high-school age is the typical one for its employment, since the immature mechanisms lend themselves very easily to such treatment. Such a procedure in no way imperils the later development of any capacity for dramatic singing. The director who uses it will find that it is ideally adapted to the attainment of homogeneity and blending and is potentially adequate to meet all the demands a growing repertoire may place upon it, which is a consummation "devoutly to be wished."

BOYS' VOICES

The boys' voice problem is, frankly, not so easy, but that fact does not limit the efficacy of the method of approach. The post-change period in the male voice is a trying one, and the production is prone to be stiff, uncertain, and tense.

Basses will be found to have grave difficulty in the region lying above *B*, middle staff, and tenors, above upper *E flat*. The rule cited above, that the heavier the lower quality, the more radical the change, is especially marked in the male voices; many instances will be found in which the singer, after straining upward for a few tones, will suddenly lose control and will either break into a falsetto or be unable to phonate at all. If the habits of production are overstrained, the falsetto may not appear, but instead only a grating sound, caused by the edges of the vocal chords chafing together.

> The practice of some teachers of allowing boys to force up the lower register is accountable for the loss of many fine voices—especially tenors who have to learn to sing their high tones easily if they are to continue to sing.[7]

At this age, therefore, the supervisor has a rare opportunity to encourage the beginning of the practice and the use of the male *mezza-voce,* or light voice, which is an indispensable feature of all mature artistic singing. A virile, vibrant quality of voice may be found occasionally, but it will unquestionably be very limited in range, and the full tones beyond *F* for tenors and *C* for basses will be so strained that the quality will be largely "yell" and the physical exertion so great that terror will look out of the eyes of the struggling vocalists. This terror of high tones is a very real thing in young men, and it is cruel not to concentrate on a technique which, if it cannot immediately develop power, can at least help to make singing something other than physical torture.

[7] A. H. Wagner, "Research in the Field of Voice Training," Music Educators National Conference, 1939.

All well-schooled male choral sections use the *mezza-voce* on pianissimo passages. There is no other means of producing a really soft, pure tone, for the physical effort entailed in attempting to squeeze down the full voice to piano proportions brings the singer very swiftly to a vocal "dead end." Naturally, the more mature and experienced the voice is in the use of the *mezza-voce,* the more controlled and smooth will be the result. There is no excuse for the failure to employ this device, which is unfortunately too infrequent of use, particularly in smaller school systems where the solution of the boys' voice problem is even more vital than in larger schools with correspondingly greater resources of natural talent.

The first step in orienting the boys in the use of the soft tone follows the pattern of approach to the girls' voices, namely, correct posture, deep breathing, and freedom from bodily tension. In addition, it is important to rid the boy of any embarrassment over breaks in the voice. Once get the student to believe that the break is only a sign that there is something behind and beyond which he has not discovered, and he will be rid of the feeling that to let the voice break is to be guilty of a grave social error.

Grouping tenors and basses by sections for short group vocalization is suggested, since this procedure lessens the sense of personal embarrassment at the queer sounds which frequently emerge from youthful throats. One should impress upon the singers that only two things are required, namely, to breathe deeply and to sing softly, assuring them that no tone is *too* soft for use. If the voice utterly fails and refuses to act, well and good—try again; but encourage the singer to refuse to make effort and to sing strictly *piano.*

The best place to begin vocalization with boys is usually just above the normal change in register, although the condition of the individual voice will sometimes call for attack either higher or lower. The *hum* followed by *oo* and *ee* on slow downward scales, as suggested for girls, is an easy way to begin the use of the *mezza-voce.* The exercises may start at

E or *F*, top staff, for tenors, and at *C* or *D flat*, middle staff, for baritones and basses. The object is to carry down the light quality as far as possible into the middle register, and to do this the tone at first must be extremely soft. The exercises may be extended upward as far as is comfortable, but care should be taken not to caricature the voice by over-loud falsetto singing, which to a growing boy may seem only silly. One should keep the routine dignified and purposive.

After a little preliminary practice, mild crescendos may be attempted, but the singer should not permit the voice to break when increasing the tone. The aim is to make the student familiar with the sensation of ease and the use of a piano dynamic. Body of tone will come later. The upper middle notes are the most difficult in all the voice to sing with freedom; *mezza-voce* exercises sung downward into the middle voice are excellent devices for easing the middle voice, as well as for building the top range.

To approach the use of the prime vowel forms, sustained successions of *ee, ay, ah, oh,* and *oo* may be used on single tones, with slight crescendos in the middle of each vowel; but as stated in the section on girls' voices, exercises are not the only means of attaining proficiency. Let melodic passages from songs also be attempted, using the hum or closed vowels for the purpose.

BASIC TONE PATTERN FOR GROUPS

In starting the repertoire training of mixed groups, one may begin by using some very quiet, sustained number, featuring half or whole tone chords, such as "O Bone Jesu," by Palestrina. It is well to begin by humming in all voices. The hum must be completely relaxed and free from strain. This can be accomplished only by humming *pianissimo*. The breathing should be quiet and deep, the throat completely free from tension. Using the consonant *n* with the lips slightly open and the tip of the tongue behind the front upper teeth helps to center the tone in the head. If the voice shows any tendency to become tense on any interval, it should be allowed to change, since the necessity either to break or to use force shows that there is tension in the throat. The goal is to hum so softly in the head that no necessity for a change in mechanism will be experienced.

After this conception of quiet dynamic has been allowed to register itself on the students' minds and voices, single vowels of *oo, ee,* and *oh* may be used for vocalizing the song—changing the vowels from time to time, but *not increasing* the dynamic. When a foundation of individual vowel production has been established on the progressions of the number, the words may be attempted; but, again, the dynamic *must remain soft.* Changing vowel forms, and particularly the *ah* sound, will at first be difficult, because of habits of tension; but with insistence upon the fundamentals of soft tone and dark vowel color, the ensemble will begin to appreciate the aim and so to sense the refinement and thrill which lie in such group technique. Once the foundation is laid, the progress should be rapid, and gradually a more firm tone, built on the fundamentals of ease and quality, will begin to emerge. The same general procedures may be used for girls' or boys' groups.

A caution should be voiced here against the too prolonged use of the vowel *oo* as a tonal pattern. It affords an admirable vehicle for fundamental procedure in establishing homogeneity of quality and freedom of tone emission, but one must not make the error of conceiving that pianissimo singing is the *final goal* in group performance. There must be a wide variety of dynamics, including the ringing crescendos which are indispensable in climactic singing, but the ability to sing pianissimo must not be sacrificed in the process.

Once having established the soft tone pattern of the initial phases of the procedure, the director should lead his singers out into the more open, resonant vowel country of *ee, ah, oh,* and *ah.* This is highly important. Henry Coward points out:

The forward tone is so easily obtained by this vowel (*oo*) that some conductors, taking the line of least resistance, use *oo* to such an extent that everything the choir sings is dominated with *oo;* consequently the dull cavernous sound spoils the effect of all their efforts.[8]

This phase of the problem will largely adjust itself if the fundamentals of soft tone have carefully been laid and if the director does not limit his group to the exclusive use of dark color.

To summarize the problem of tone production, then, we deem it wise to quote from an address by the late Frank Beach to the Music Supervisors National Conference in 1932. The address, though not long, was none the less rather epochal in character and has had frequent quotation, whole or in part.

The purpose is to urge the use of the legitimate soft tone as a foundation upon which to build a better vocal quality; one that will be adequate to meet the varying demands of the best choral music. The director who utilizes the soft tone as a basis to which he returns frequently for his measurement of quality will discover the full singing voice will grow surprisingly in intensity and resonance. By soft tone, we mean a light, floating tone that is truly vibrant and so supported on the breath that it may be sustained without wavering in pitch; a tone that is piano in dynamic intensity and so freely produced that it may be increased without change in quality. This of course is a perfect tone; but such must be the ideal of the conductor who would achieve beautiful and vital effects in choral singing. This ideal is essential because:

1. The full resonant tone which is rightly produced can be none other than the soft tone, increased in resonance and power.

2. The soft tone, produced as it must be, on a finely balanced breath, encourages freedom from strain and tension.

3. The ideal soft tone affords an effective means for developing that most important tonal characteristic—accurate intonation.

4. The soft tone makes defects in vowel color readily apparent.

5. Its use affords a safe procedure in the development of upper tones, and furnishes a solution for the problem of increasing the tenor section of the chorus.

[8] Henry Coward, *Choral Technique and Interpretation,* London: Novello and Co.; H. W. Gray Co., New York, Sole Agents for the U. S. A., p. 26.

6. It makes for a uniform type of production, through the dynamic range of the singing voice.[9]

This suggested approach to the problem of tone production is a much slower and more meticulous process than the "shout and sing" method, but every step gained will renew and increase itself many times in the developing technique, and each new number in the repertoire will be vastly easier and more zestful because of the basic habits built into its predecessors.

The gist of the whole tone production matter, therefore, lies in the acceptance of a standard which measures vocal sound in terms of quality rather than quantity, which automatically accedes to the principle that over-loud dynamics in the high-school age are incompatible with refined tone, and that ease of production and beauty of quality are inseparable correlates in all stages and types of group singing.

[9] Frank Beach, "The Legitimate Soft Tone in Singing," Music Educators National Conference, 1932.

CHAPTER SIX

Performance

➤➤➤➤—◀◀◀◀

*Music is essentially an act of ut-
terance. It was created to be performed by somebody to somebody.**

➤➤➤➤—◀◀◀◀

IN the field of performance we come at last to the final testing ground of true musical values. Here the concepts, emotions, and technical drill, which have been developed in the
training period, are brought to fruition, and their coordinate
result marks the degree of artistic excellence which has been
achieved. Initial public performances, however, do not irrev-
ocably set the standard of any given group, for elements of
nerve tension, acoustical surroundings, and varying types of
audiences have marked effect upon all units. Even granting
that the training has been orthodox in all particulars, it is
necessary that groups have comprehensive experience before
the public if they are faithfully to disclose the quality of
musical technique and discipline which have furnished the
background for their preparation. Naturally, the more detailed and painstaking the drill, the less serious will be the
detrimental effect of local conditions on performance, and the
more accelerated will be the development before the public.

An interesting and beneficent phenomenon, with which
many groups and directors are thoroughly familiar, exists in applied effort before an audience. It is that under the stimulus
of public performance a unit may rise to heights of excellence
which the rehearsal periods have never been able to produce.
Keyed to a high level of concentration and sensitive response,
an ensemble may, in the hands of an imaginative conductor,
be made to produce startling effects under such conditions—
effects which are born of the moment and which, regardless of

* James L. Mursell, *Music in American Schools*, Boston: Silver Burdette,
1943, p. 294. (*By special permission of the publishers.*)

like conditions, may never exactly be reproduced in succeeding efforts. Nothing is more thrilling than this pursuit of elusive, subtle moods in the heat of successive performance. Such experiences do not nullify nor lessen the necessity for basic, studied drill; they merely sublimate it and fuse both group and conductor into a unit for fascinating flights into the intangible realm of pure aesthetic emotion.

Such experiences register their greatest good upon the performers themselves. Those who listen will, of course, if they are in rapport with this idiom of expression, be strongly moved; but it remains for those who have patiently built the basic fundamentals into the work to reap a harvest of group and individual expression which, in its elevation of the spirit, is immeasurable, and which time is impotent to eradicate. These moments are like a flight into the stratosphere, or a descent into unfathomed depths of sea. They can be essayed only after long and assiduous preparation during which no element which may be necessary for success can be slighted or overlooked. If such is not the character of the foundations, the adventure is bound to result in disaster or to fall short of its aim.

Unfortunately, there are many directors who depend too much upon the inspiration of the climactic moment to supply magically the qualities which the training has not stressed. They can but fail, for inspiration has power only to build loftier structures upon foundations already laid. Inspiration cannot instantaneously create technical foundations on which to rear its temples. The result of such a philosophy may be likened to the chaotic daubs of a would-be painter who, knowing the technique of neither the palette nor the brush, attempts to portray a landscape without a comprehensive knowledge of color and line.

Tone quality is a basic fundamental of worthy applied performance, as we have seen in the preceding chapter. With this fact in mind we shall now turn to other factors which must be present if standards of excellence in rendition are to be attained. In the main they lie in the fields of *intonation, diction, tempo, phrasing,* and *dynamics.* With these successively we now shall deal.

INTONATION

Accurate intonation in singing is the result of proper co-ordination between the productive organism and the ear. Both must function properly if correct pitch is to be maintained. An individual may have true pitch perception, but through tension in the voice production or local inflammation, his vocalization may not be true of intonation. If the ear is at fault, the intonation is bound to be inaccurate. At times inaccurate intonation is the result of inexperience and may be remedied by training, but there are cases in which the auditory nerves are insensible to tonal variation, and in such instances very little progress can be made. Most people have normal pitch perception, and their impure intonation may be largely due to improper vocalization. At times conditions outside the individual cause difficulty and affect the intonation. For instance, a room with low ceiling and poor acoustical properties, or an overheated auditorium may cause the tone to flat, whereas a large, echoing auditorium is almost sure to produce sharpness. Physical fatigue and nerve tension are other factors which may be counted on to cause difficulty, and the efficient director will learn to differentiate between external local conditions and internal fundamental ones which affect intonation; he will take steps to overcome them, for notwithstanding the presence of other laudable qualities, if the intonation is faulty, artistry has fled.

Much of the difficulty in group intonation is simply the result of a lack of interval consciousness and sufficient drill in the all-important function of tuning. No ensemble can be expected to sing with true intonation until all sections can vocalize their individual parts accurately without accompaniment. This calls for painstaking, patient drill, which, unless carried out in the proper attitude on the part of both director and students, may become monotonous and disintegrating. A spirit of enthusiasm and encouragement in leadership will create zest for pitch infallibility on the part of the singers, and the consciousness of growth will act as an incentive to develop that fundamental accuracy which is indispensable.

AIDS IN DEVELOPING ACCURATE INTONATION

Various devices may be used to develop pure intonation. The inner parts are the ones most subject to error. These must be rehearsed independently until they can be sung as individual cantus, or fitted into the harmonic pattern with complete accuracy. There is no short cut to the attainment of exactness in singing progressions. Wherever the inaccuracy occurs, there the director and singers must patiently concentrate their efforts until all uncertainties are eliminated. Nine times in ten a group will sing a thoroughly familiar tune in pitch. Hence, if the ranges of a four-part composition are within the normal limit of the voices, it requires only complete familiarity of all the parts with their respective scores to bring tonal order out of chaos. If the unit is young and inexperienced, it may be necessary to work out the individual parts with the aid of a piano, but the sooner the piano as a crutch can be dispensed with, the better.

In young a cappella groups, during the preliminary routine of learning the score, the piano may sound chords on the initial beats of alternate measures and later at the attack of phrases or periods, thus giving the various sections a constant mechanical check on their accuracy. Teaching the ensemble to sing successions of tonic, subdominant and dominant chords in various keys helps to build a consciousness of intervals which readily adapts itself to chordal tuning in the repertoire.

As the various voice parts of the number develop, the successive chords may be sustained in order that the tonality may become firmly fixed in mind. A cappella singing should be stressed in all groups, even though the selection may call for an accompaniment, as such a technique is vital to the development of independence and pure harmonization. The thrill of learning to produce a continuity of harmonizing voice parts on pitch is highly stimulating; it raises the level of concept in the ensemble from that in which the singers strive merely to execute a given voice part with accuracy, to one in which every note, subordinate or melodic, is essential to the evolution of a choral pattern that is woven from the blended strands of tone emanating from each section.

Consonant harmony, of course, is comparatively easy, but dissonance, suspended harmonies, and passing notes call for meticulous exactness and must be rehearsed until the unrest which they portray is as sure of concept as the simplest consonant harmonies.

The difficulties of pure intonation in groups are infinitely increased by reason of the fact that each individual voice must be in tune with its section, each section with the others, and, in accompanied singing, the whole in tune with the instrument and the key. In a cappella performance the section carrying the melodic line may develop sharpness or flatness, or a subordinate section may go astray; if the sense of chordal harmony is strong, the other sections may accommodate their own voice line to the error, if it is prolonged. In other words, they flat or sharp together. This is naturally less distressing to the hearer than the chaotic condition which occurs when one part errs and the others are unable to follow into the bypaths. But the intervals during which successive new fundamental pitches are being established, in the first case, are periods of anxiety on the part of conductor, singers, and audience; the results are always so unpredictable and hazardous that the director emerges from such an adventure with moist brow and a sense of narrowly averted tonal disaster. Individual and collective insurance against this type of transgression is essential.

Some a cappella pitch difficulties are caused by the inability of the group to maintain the voice ranges of the composition. In such cases it is wise either to choose a selection which is within the pitch range of the ensemble, or, if the effectiveness of the piece is not thereby too severely jeopardized, to lower the key a half or whole step, thus bringing it into the range level of the unit. There is also the device of interchanging alto and tenor parts when certain phrases in the tenor are beyond the working range of that section; but no ensemble, either inexperienced or seasoned, should be subjected to the ordeal of attempting to sustain, at pitch, music which is over their heads in difficulty. There are instances, also, in which the elevation of the key may prove the answer to a knotty pitch problem. A cappella singing is so definitely a project of group harmony within any given key that experimentation above and below the original are not only salutary discipline but sound technique, and such alteration of key many times results in achievement of a freedom from pitch difficulty which is a coveted boon.

It should be remembered that the best insurance against poor intonation lies, first, in correct voice production—the soft, floating tone which affords so excellent a "means for the development of that most important tonal characteristic—accurate pitch;" [1] second, in complete mastery of the score. If these two elements are present, the remaining causes of pitch inaccuracy lie in conditions that lend themselves to easy remedy. If either or both of them are basically at fault, no general conditioning theraphy can be expected to bring about the desired results until they are corrected.

Let it be granted, then, that there is no substitute for accurate intonation; that it must be individual, sectional, and unitary; that its greatest glory is achieved when singing is unaccompanied. If the written accompaniment which is provided is merely a duplicate of the voice parts, it may be eliminated. If it provides a background essential to the choral picture, the pitch independence of the well-drilled group will permit its function as the adornment for which it was created, and as which it only can be effective.

[1] Beach, *op. cit.*

DICTION

In the element of diction in ensemble singing we have the medium by which we transform abstract tone into linguistic forms and so convey the exact meaning of music and text to the hearer. Instrumental music has expressive power, some of it highly potent; but unless it be programme music, or imitative, its message and meaning will be largely abstract and as varied as the number of its individual listeners. The type of instrument or ensemble and the pattern of the music itself will combine to create mental and emotional reaction, depending upon the artistry of the score, the quality of performance, and the musical intelligence and receptivity of the individual auditor. In vocal music, however, the score and phonation processes are designed to give expression to a text. Although the craftsmanship of the composition and the quality of performance vitally affect the emotional response, here we have the additional factor of a definite literary form, the level of which has a profound bearing on the result, and around which the whole musical process revolves.

Pure intonation is fundamental, as we have seen, and good tone quality is the vital phonation medium for any high-grade choral expression. It follows logically that if the diction is to achieve its true purpose, it must utilize refined quality that is true to pitch. Refined quality and diction are coordinate and interdependent; that is, good diction induces good quality, and vice versa. There would be no purpose in trying to develop a refined, basic tone quality if it could not be used in articulation.

Successful singing diction should have two characteristics: first, naturalness and fidelity to the given language; and second, distinctness and clarity. When we say that the diction must be natural, we do not mean that it should typify the common speech of the average individual. The diction of the street and of the common day, when transferred into song, becomes hard, crude, angular, and defiant of good tone quality. What we mean by naturalness is that the auditor in listening to the text will be unconscious of any foreignness of accent or emphasis, or of any affected mannerisms in pronunciation which may affect reception of the message of the words. When we speak of distinctness, we mean that every syllable, word, and phrase must be clearly intelligible to the listener without any apparent effort to make them so. Actually, a great deal of mental effort and emphasis, as well as complete coordination of the organs of articulation, must go into the performance if the results to the auditor are to be satisfactory. Consistently intelligible pronunciation is of prime importance because without it the listener has no clue to the animating source of the music. The composer's music is what it is because the words suggested it.

But why is singing diction different from common speech, and why the need for careful and prolonged drill on vowel and consonant articulation if, in the end, the effect is to be as nearly like refined speech as possible? The reason is not far to seek. Singing is higher and louder than speech; it is sustained and prolonged, and in this sustentation and prolongation it must so faithfully preserve the outlines of accent, vowel, and consonant values that no abbreviations or exaggerations are apparent.

VOWELS

Singing, in its last simple analysis, is merely sustained pronunciation to musical pitch. One cannot open his mouth and vocalize a sound without utilizing some vowel form. The pleasantness of the result is dependent upon the manner in which that vowel form is pronounced or phonated. Consonants are interruptions in the sustained flow of vowel sound, and these interruptions take the form of stoppages of various kinds and locations, which, preceding and following the various vowel forms, give meaning and intelligence to the syllables. Speech is rapid, unsustained, and crisp, with the shortest possible time given for the pronunciation of the vowels. The mouth is uniformly much more closed than in singing, and, except in schooled utterance, the consonants too frequently are only partially articulated.

Singing forms a chain of vowels, the links typifying the vowels and the couplings forming the consonants. No consonant at any time is prolonged, unless it be for a deliberate effect. Moreover, functions of the consonant and vowel must be kept strictly separate. Any encroachment on a vowel by a consonant causes adulteration of the vowel. It is the failure completely to separate the two functions which creates so much havoc in the diction of singers and of speakers. Beauty of tone quality is vested in the vowel; distinctness in the correct articulation of the consonant.

CONDENSATION OF VOWEL SOUNDS

Since the vowel is the medium of tone extension, it follows that the fewer the forms into which we can compress our total vocal needs, the more uniform will be our tone color and the simpler our technique. Concentration of activity into the fewest possible divisions compatible with efficiency is a coveted goal in all life's processes. In singing it is no less an aim. In fact, it is vital, for the fewer the number of fundamental positions which the vocal organism is compelled to use, the surer and more definite will those positions be, and the easier will be the phonation. In addition to the five prime vowels of the English language there are modifications of each which make a total of many times that number. It is patent that no singer or chorus can achieve homogeneity of tone quality throughout the voice range without reducing this total very drastically. Fortunately, in singing, many of the minor vowel forms occur on unaccented syllables and are not prolonged, thus simplifying the task of preserving uniform, pleasing quality and at the same time of remaining distinct.

Italian is the simplest and most ideal language for singing, for the reason that the vowel forms are fewer than in any other language; also the succession of consonants between vowels encountered in other languages is unknown to it. Moreover, Italian gives each vowel its pure, prime sound, sustaining it to its full duration, and sharply separating it from the consonant—which is very crisply articulated—thereby adding luster and solidity to the contrasting vowel.

In choral singing we can do no better than to pattern our diction after the example of the Italians. First of all, we should reduce to a minimum the number of vowel sounds which we employ in singing. It is amazing how much a trained singer can accomplish with the five prime sounds of *ah, ay, ee, oh,* and *oo.* Through the correct articulation of the consonants he can make practically any English text crystal clear to the hearer with only a minimum use of the partials. Too frequently in choral singing we hear a wide variety of vowel sounds, many of which, being only partials, are hard for any vocalist to produce with ease, much less with good quality, and we fail to hear a complete articulation of the consonant; instead we hear a mixture of the consonant and vowel functions and an adulteration of the tone quality.

In order to make our purpose clear, it should be said that the condensation of vowel sounds here suggested is not proposed in a spirit of indifference toward the demands of purity in English pronunciation. Cultured speech should meticulously enforce all the subtleties of vowel form which are necessary if the full beauties of our vernacular are to be preserved. However, it should be remembered that we are dealing with song, which, as stated above, is a succession of vowel sounds. To be successful these vowel sounds must be not only distinct; they must be agreeable, nay, beautiful. The further away we get from the primary vowel sounds, the more we endanger the quality; this fact is simply due to the laws governing the emission of the singing tone. Vowels in singing suspension are very different from those in speech. Every singer knows that even in the five prime sounds he has more difficulty in the production of some than he does with others. Moreover, the ascent

68

or descent of the scale calls for certain modifications of vowel forms to accommodate the necessary adjustments in throat and larynx.

We cannot sing intelligently and with distinctness in the English language without preserving its fundamental vowel forms, but we can so regulate our singing diction that we stay as close as possible to the prime vowel sounds without caricaturing the language in any degree. The ideal result is obtained when the hearer is conscious of no adulterations or eccentricities and when the singer forms each sound according to the laws governing correct emission—utilizing the consonants fully —thus making the performance both distinct and natural.

For example, the words "calm," "not," and "night" may well be sung with the same prime fundamental sound of *ah*. If the consonants are well articulated, there is no sacrifice of distinctness, no violation of the language, and the gain is with the singer who is thus enabled to make one fundamental position answer for three sounds.

VOWEL ATTACK

The manner of starting vowel sounds in singing (called the attack) is highly important both to the soloist and to the ensemble. In the section on "Breathing" the act of phonation was described as the result of vibrations of the vocal bands, caused by their resistance to the breath. The bands should not come into actual physical contact but should approximate so closely that only the amount of air necessary for the stimulation of the correct number of vibrations is allowed to escape. Hence, the breath is responsible not only for sufficient supply of air to maintain the vibrations but also for adequate pressure to regulate the *extent* of these vibrations which, through resonance reinforcement, determine the size of the tone.

In the ideal attack of a vowel sound the start of the tone should be clear and incisive, squarely in the center of the tone target. A common error in attack occurs when the chords actually come into contact with each other before the start of the tone and must be forced apart by the breath. This causes a clucking sound commonly referred to as the *glottis stroke*. The term is really a misnomer, as the old masters referred to the *perfect attack* as the *stroke of the glottis*. The effect of the so-called *glottis stroke* is both unpleasant and harmful, for the error easily becomes a habit and is irritating to the edges of the vocal bands. When successions of vowels are encountered in a singing text, in such expressions as "to all," "we are," "who are," etc., singers are prone either to attack the *second* vowel with a *glottis stroke* or to insert an extra consonant between them, as "to (w)all," "we (y) are," "who (w)are." Such errors present a real problem to the director who would make the diction of his units pure. A definite break between the vowels may prevent the unsavory *w* or *y*, but interruptions of the melodic line are potentially damaging to the *sustenuto*. Some directors seek to solve the difficulty by schooling the singers in the use of an interpolated soft *h* between the vowels, the theory being that, in time, the crutch may be dispensed with or rendered inaudible, leaving the attack of the second vowel clear and true. Vocalization, on a unison pitch, of sustained successions of prime vowel sounds—free from the *glottis stroke* and on the pure impulse of the breath—are help-ful. This should be followed by the practice of pattern phrases from the text which feature the problem, carrying over into the words the neat joining of vowels established through the medium of the exercise. In time the singers should learn, as must the soloist, to attack successions of vowels, either in legato or in broken passages, with the purity which correct singing demands.

Another error in attack is the reverse of the *glottis stroke*. In this case free air is allowed to escape before the vocal bands assume their correct approximation, resulting in the *aspirated* or *breathy* attack. Such a fault should be corrected, as it is wasteful of the breath and greatly diminishes clarity. Its treat-ment consists in attacking the tone while seeming to suspend the breath entirely. In earlier days singing masters instructed their students to hold a lighted candle before their lips while singing. If the candle flickered or was extinguished, the singer knew he was wasting breath. In attempting to correct the breathy attack, one must be careful to avoid the opposite extreme, i.e., the *glottis stroke*.

Still another common faulty attack is the so-called *scoop*. In this the singer, instead of attacking the tone fairly in the center, slurs or glides into it from below. Upper tones are most likely to fall victim to this habit, but wherever it occurs, the practice should be corrected, as it is one of the Peck's Bad Boys of singing.

DIPHTHONGS

In song, each syllable must have only one fundamental vowel sound. This cannot be stressed too strongly. The habit of sustaining both sounds on diphthongs is a vicious one and should never be countenanced. Regardless of the number of notes assigned to the vowel, the fundamental or long sound is the only one to be sustained. One must instinctively know what the fundamental sound is at sight and must preserve it throughout the duration of the syllable. Such words as "night" (nah-eet), "quite" (qah-eet), "where" (wheh-ur), "dear" (dee-ur), and "dew" (dee-oo) are cardinal offenders to the uninitiated. Whether the secondary sound comes before the long one, as in "dew," or after it, as in "night," the short sound must not be sustained; it must be glided over in the attack, or be allowed to vanish with the final expiration of the long sound.

If the basic soft dynamic in tone production is insisted upon, the whole vowel problem is infinitely simplified; for, as has been pointed out, the soft tone makes defects in vowel color readily apparent. In singing the vowels, *the jaw should be completely relaxed, thus insuring that the mouth is amply open for the various forms, and the tongue tip should lie comfortably behind the lower teeth. The lips should be mobile and free to shape themselves easily to the need of the vowel.*

71

FUNDAMENTALS OF CHORAL EXPRESSION

TREATMENT OF VARIOUS VOWEL PROBLEMS

A simple means of improving an unsatisfactory vowel sound is to suggest some other vowel color to be blended with it, or to suggest that it be sung more in the mold of some other vowel form. This is like mixing colors on a canvas; if one is too sharp or harsh, it can be relieved by the addition of a neutralizing agent through the use of one or more additional colors. Hence, if the tone quality on such words as "man" or "can" is offensively thin, the broader quality of the short Italian *a* may be suggested. The difficulty of such sounds as the short *a*, short *e*, and short *i* arises from the necessity of sustaining them in singing. In speech they are not offensive because they are usually of short duration; but when they are sustained in song, they become disturbing unless they are made to partake of the color of the nearest prime sound. Some directors prefer to meet the problem by simply suggesting a more open mouth on such sounds, but extreme dropping of the jaw on these vowels may lead to exaggerations that are scarcely less objectionable than the original fault.

The long *e* sound is one of the most intense colors we have. When correctly sung, it has great beauty and is conducive to resonance. Care should be taken that it is not directed too much toward the front teeth, but rather that it is given a deep, rich, sonorous sound, borrowed somewhat from the *oo,* with lips slightly rounded. Ensembles should cultivate such darker shadings to offset the thin unvocal quality so characteristic of juvenile speech. At times young singers are prone to pronounce the final *es* as though it were spelled *uz:* "rosuz," "gladnuss," "kissuz," etc. Fortunately, this is a crudity that is not very frequent, but the tendency should be sharply corrected whenever found.

A very common habit in unskilled groups is to give the syllables *er, ar, ur, ir,* a consonant rather than a vowel sound, and the result is a guttural *r,* which is formed by a stiff tongue root and an almost complete obliteration of the vowel itself.

In combating this error we must remember, again, that each syllable is allotted but one fundamental sound, and that that sound must be *vowel*. In all such syllables the vowel should be sung as though no following consonant were present, and, coincident with the completion of its time value, the *r* should be formed with a neat flip of the tip of the tongue. Thus *ur* or *er* may be sung as *uh-r* and *ar* as *ah-r*. If there is concentration on the vowel sound, the consonant will assume its rightful position on the last impulse of the pronounciation.

In the singing of the short *i* we frequently hear a sound which tends too much toward short *e*. This may be corrected by the use of long *e* quality, which in speech may sound exaggerated, but which in singing may be the means of giving the tone that depth and richness which it needs. On final syllables of *ing* particularly, the sound in untrained ensembles is prone to become almost *eng* with a childish, thin quality which is unpleasant. All such tendencies may be corrected by persistent use of the long *e* quality. In fact, the use of long *e* color on all suffixes of *ing*, or on syllables in which the short *i* is followed by *m* or *n* is sound technique.

In summarizing vowel production, let it be the aim to preserve a uniform, soft quality which prevents the emergence of harsh, ungraceful tones, and which puts a premium upon purity and ease. This does not mean that it should be the aim to make all vowels sound alike. It does mean, however, that if homogeneity of quality is preserved as a fundamental objective, the singers will be able to achieve mellow tone color and ease even in the more brilliant vowel forms which are so vital to the tonal color scheme. Most of the objectionable vowel quality encountered in choral groups is the result of over-singing or of muscular tension. Insistence upon a soft dynamic will help enormously toward guiding both singers and directors toward the desired ends. *If the tongue is kept forward so that the throat and the palate may be free to do their work unhampered by the tongue base, the jaw com-*

pletely relaxed, and the mouth fully opened, a physical back-ground should thereby be created which is conducive to the development of uniformly satisfactory tone color. Ease in the production of the limited number of vowel forms necessary for the textual demands of any normal repertoire will naturally follow.

CONSONANTS

What of the consonants? The use of this very important element in diction is a subject of much controversy and dispute; but a great deal of the difficulty which directors encounter in dealing with the consonants is due to ignorance of their vital function and of their capacity to facilitate rather than hinder purity of articulation and commendable tone quality. Some directors seek to soften and eliminate the consonants on the theory that they are interruptions and obstructions to the tone flow; therefore, they argue that the more they are reduced and neutralized, the less will they interfere with the vowel forms. Though this theory may seem to the uninitiated to be sound logic, the opposite is actually the case.

OPPOSING FUNCTIONS OF VOWELS AND CONSONANTS

As indicated earlier in this section, the vowels and consonants have opposing functions. Vowels are the result of free and unhampered streams of vibrations set in motion by the edges of the vocal chords. Consonants are definitely designed to create varying types of obstruction and interference, preceding or following vowels, thus giving our phonation a series of patterns which provide means of communication between humankind. In singing and in speech we have a wide variety of sound interruptions; in order to be intelligible these interruptions must be clear, definite, and faithful to their own functional realm. When we sharply separate consonant and vowel functions, we have coordinating, opposing forces which, through their very opposition, give to each a startling clarity, solidity, and emphasis which create a sense of freedom and well-being in the singer or speaker. This brings satisfaction to the listener which comes from a diction that leaves nothing to be desired.

NECESSITY FOR COMPLETE ARTICULATION

There is then nothing to fear from clear-cut consonant articulation. In fact, the more crisply and completely the consonants are pronounced, the more salutary will be the effect upon the contrasting vowel. The effect of good consonant articulation on the vowel may be likened to the momentary obstruction of a spring freshet, which leaps forward with renewed energy and abandon once it is released. Most consonants are formed through the twofold action of stoppage and release, both of which must be present if we are to have distinctness. It is the omission of the release which results in so much indistinct articulation in speech and song. Failure to follow through with the consonant is fraught with as evil results as it is with the golfer. Again, just as the golfer must stay in place until the stroke is finished. so must the consonant forbear from unduly leaning over on the following vowel or syllable.

For instance, the consonant *d* is formed by stopping the sound at the hard palate, followed by a sub-vocal *uh* as it is released. If the release is unvocalized, the consonant can be recognized only by implication. When, in singing, *d* is followed by a vowel, as in "and all," the vowel may automatically provide the release necessary for distinctness without our being required to sing " and *uh* all."

When, however, we have final and initial consonants on adjacent syllables, as in "drink to," there must be a slight *uh* of release on the *k,* or a momentary suspension of breath between the consonants if our diction is to be clear.

At times a final consonant is entirely omitted, and we hear

"an night," instead of "and night," or a final *s* is carried over to ludicrous effect, as in "lettus spray" for "let us pray." Such examples of bad articulation are not exaggerated; they are too common, as most directors know, and the whole sorry mess is largely due to the failure to "follow through" on the consonant, or to keep it in its place. R. J. Peterson says:

> When one contemplates the prevailing carelessness in consonant articulation of the average choral group, one is forced to the conclusion that most of the words of our language are only half complete.[2]

Clusters of consonants, which are often encountered, accentuate the difficulty of obtaining clarity without sacrificing the sustained singing line. In such situations *ample time* must be given for articulation if the consonants are to fulfill their function. Henry Coward, the eminent English choir master, has his singers vocalize—very softly—the release of such consonants with the sound of *uh*.[3] For example, "Help Lord" is sung "Help (uh) Lord," the *uh* naturally being timed to synchronize with the release of the *p*. Likewise the Italian vegetable man may say "you bet -ta my life" to our amusement, but he is only being true to his native language which calls for the release of its consonants with a resounding smack!

The *th* is a cardinal offender and is conspicuous by its absence in average choral diction. Coward again says, "the choir that can sing *th* perfectly is in the highest class."[4] Such details loom large in group singing because of the great frequency of their occurence.

The whole problem of the consonants is largely one of *discipline and timing*. Casual American speech is notoriously slovenly in articulation and our vocal mechanisms become lethargic from inertia. Consonants *require time and energy* for *their complete articulation* and they cannot be expected to

[2] R. J. Peterson, "The Unaccompanied Choir," Music Educators National Conference, 1937.
[3] Coward, *op. cit.*, p. 85.
[4] *Idem.*

survive on the half-ration of each which is commonly allotted them. Only strict self-discipline can develop resistance
to the half-articulation which is a national habit.

Consonants are the war horses of our language; if correctly formed, they cannot be overworked. In ensembles they are
best when exaggerated. When attacked clearly and cleanly,
they furnish a prime means of establishing and maintaining
rythm—the most expressive single element in music. They
depict drama, pathos, awe, and gaiety by the simple means of
emphasis; but without their sparkling clarity, the whole choral
landscape becomes swathed in foggy mist.

We must, then, completely articulate our consonants, which
means that we must exaggerate them about fifty per cent above
our average careless speech. When "cold" becomes icy from
the breath of the passing consonants, when "holy" and
"heavenly" become instantly associated in the minds of our
hearers with the celestial—because of the powerful suggestion
lodged in the emphatic *h*—we shall begin to sense the thrill
that lies in truly articulate diction; we shall come to know a
new and more wholesome respect for the beauty of our
language. Through singing we shall be improving our speech
and so be contributing to better general speech habits and a
cultured address, which is so vital to the personality of every
individual.

TEMPO

In addition to being a master dramatist and poet, William
Shakespeare must have been a music critic of no mean ability
and discernment, for he says in *King Richard II*:

> How sour sweet music is
> When time is broke and no proportion kept!

If it were given to the famous bard to hear some of the choral
performances of our current generation, one wonders whether
the resources of his rich vocabulary would be sufficient to

describe the futility of the efforts of many directors to find the tempo which most aptly expresses the spirit and mood of the music they conduct.

Before music of any type existed, there was rhythm; for emotions that could not be restrained, savages found expression in various dances accompanied by pulsating cries or by the monotonous beat of a tom-tom. Through the ages this cardinal element of rhythm has been throbbing like the pulse of a cosmic heart; and all of life in countless ways is inexorably tuned to its beat. It is not surprising, therefore, that rhythm and tempo should head the list of expressive elements in music.

No matter how potentially stirring a march may be in the score, it does not become a march until it is performed in the quick-step fashion of its type. If played in slow motion, it becomes a dirge, a melancholy musical antithesis of the original.

IMPORTANCE OF CORRECT MUSIC TEMPO

Rhythm is the regular recurrence of musical accent; tempo is the speed of the rhythm, and it is this rate of speed which is so powerful an expressive quality in music that all other phases of interpretation draw their vitality from it. Hollis Dann maintains:

> . . . The ability to indicate the correct tempo and variations of tempo is altogether the most important duty of the conductor. It requires careful study, much experience and musical background. There is no short cut to the attainment of this power.[5]

Perhaps the greatest asset to the establishment of correct tempo in choral music is an innate singing sense on the part of the conductor. If he is a singer or has had thorough vocal study, his vocal intuitions should be reasonably accurate. Intuitions are not enough, however, and the choral conductor must use all the means available to make his choice of tempo the correct one for the given piece.

[5] Hollis Dann, *Conductor's Book,* New York: American Book Co., 1936, p. 66.

Metronome markings, when indicated, are designed for his aid and should be regarded as mandatory when present. Many numbers have no such tempo indication, and then the conductor must fall back upon the music terminology. Unfortunately, this is not an altogether accurate means of determining tempos, for there are several speeds in the realm of each term. At best such terms are a relative indication of the basic speed which the composer desired.

There is also the matter of the tradition of the piece. This is valuable, provided the number *has* a tradition, and provided the instructor has heard it, and provided the rendition he heard was authentic. Many of the classics, of course, have traditional tempos, but if renditions of them are not available on records, the possibility of hearing them authentically performed is somewhat remote.

What is there left to fall back on? First, there is the text. Of course, if the text of Lotti's exquisite "Surely He Hath Bourne Our Griefs" occasions no different emotional reaction in the director from that of Purcell's "In These Delightful Pleasant Groves," the quest for artistic expression is over before it is begun. Fortunately, the majority of directors are not so emotionally opaque; and serious study of the spirit of the text, the era of its conception, and its varying moods should moor the conductor in the vicinity, at least, of the correct timing.

Then there is the music itself. All choral music, if it be worthy and not merely a melodic jingle-jangle, is designed to mirror the spirit and mood of the text which inspired it. Choral music is not first composed, later to have the text superimposed upon it—unless perchance it be some misguided arrangement of MacDowell's "To a Wild Rose," or, in the words of Irving Kolodin, of that musical nausea, Liszt's "Liebestraum." The score, then, is authentically a musical voicing of the text, and no sensitive or experienced director can fail to feel the inherent motion of a score when it is considered as a unit with the text. His concept may vary a little from that of a colleague, but if he seeks earnestly and tries honestly—not being afraid to experiment a bit in the fascinating realm of timing—he will emerge, *sometime,* with a tempo that "fits," based on the background and spirit of the piece and on his studious deduction of the composer's intent.

VARIATIONS OF TEMPO

Having ascertained the basic speed of the piece through any or all of the means cited above, the director must not consider the matter closed, for there remain all the embroideries of tempo rubato, retard, and accelerando, which must be added if the piece is to have the variety, nuance, and expressiveness which are always latent in choral performance.

Metronomes are not imaginative instruments; they are mechanical, and hence to maintain rigidity of rhythmic outline as set by the metronome is to err in the manner of a sixth-grade lad who might read the "Charge of the Light Brigade." On the one hand we have the necessity of maintaining an ever on-going motion, for melody is horizontal; it is always on the move forward, and "song must push on to its inevitable end"! [6]

On the other hand, the ceaseless pounding of pulse is destructive of the very essence of freedom which must breathe in the notes of our singing. Frederick Chopin's "Rain-drop Prelude" is a musical description of a fevered dream in which single drops of rain fell in unending rhythmic monotony on the composer's forehead, driving him to madness and despair.

Tempo rubato is the modification of the steady rhythm of music through the prolongation or acceleration of certain notes. It is thus a means of avoiding the monotony of rigid speeds and rhythm; it offers a subtle means of emphasizing certain phases of the text as well as of enhancing the charm and effectiveness of the music. Care must be taken that the rubato be not overindulged to the extent that it becomes too much an over-all pattern. Like so many other elements

[6] H. P. Green, *Interpretation in Song,* London: Macmillan and Co., 1934, p. 43.

in music which are admirable in themselves, if it is carried to extremes, it becomes a definite fault.

AIDS IN SECURING PROPER TEMPO

Along this portion of the choral director's pilgrimage there are a few guideposts which are worthy of careful attention. Among them may be noted the following:

1. There must be the capacity to hold the given tempo and rhythmic pulse without variations—as a basis on which to mould alterations of tempo demanded by the music and text.

2. Not all of the given piece may call for the same basic tempo, but whenever an accelerando, or a retard, or a rubato is used, there must be a prompt and definite return to *a tempo*.

3. Tempos of amateur groups are more often too slow than too fast. The village choir which intones, "Seated one day at the organ," at a lugubrious grave is not portraying a restless, soul-weary organist; long before the "grand amen," his cares have ceased to fret him, and he and the audience have been musically interred. Beware of lost motion which endangers life and expression in the music.

4. The experience and ability of the group have much to do with its effectiveness at high speeds. If a brisk allegro taxes the technique of the young ensemble, one should not achieve mere speed at the cost of quality or distinctness. A group must become seasoned to a fast tempo before it can be at ease or effective in it.

5. Cumulative, long-drawn-out retards are hazardous. It is better to set a slower tempo for the duration of the retard and then to stick to it. The power of pulse and speed is so potent that even *one beat* sung out of the pattern is significant.

6. The director should begin accelerandos, retards, or rubatos on accented beats, and take up the *a tempo* likewise. He should keep all effects rhythmically intact.

7. The conductor should avoid at all costs the habit of automatically singing pianissimo passages slower than tempo. To do so invites a group of choral ills that it is well to avoid.

FUNDAMENTALS OF CHORAL EXPRESSION

These suggestions may furnish a basis for further investigation and experimentation by the director. They are, of necessity, general, for every piece of music has its own personality as definitely as have those who sing it; thorough acquaintance with a personality is essential if it is to be understood. The whole matter of tempo and rhythm should be delivered into the director's hands labeled CAUTION, DYNAMITE, HANDLE WITH CARE.

PHRASING

A phrase in music is a portion of a theme or melody having a certain balance within itself, but it is incomplete without the remainder of the theme. In speech it is any brief, pithy expression which contains a single idea. Phrasing in choral music is too often considered as denoting intervals at which breath is taken. It is obvious that wherever pauses occur in singing, breath will automatically be inhaled and that such pauses should occur at logical suspensions of the text and music; but to limit one's conception of the phrase to that of a utility stop for refueling is to miss the primary significance of a phase of performance which is an art in itself.

PHRASING FOR BREATH

First, let us consider briefly the matter of breathing as it relates to phrasing and then treat the broader aspects of this element of interpretation. In any text there are constantly recurring pauses which are the natural result of the literary form. At all of these it is impossible for the singer not to breathe unless he deliberately wills not to do so, or is so instructed by the director. At rests, then, it may be granted that breath will be available. If the textual phrase is longer than a single individual breath is able to compass, there are other means of reinforcement without breaking the phrase for that purpose. One means lies in the complete articulation of final consonants. When there is a thorough "follow through" on the consonant, and the dual elements of stoppage and release are

82

present, there is an automatic rebound of the diaphragm, which, though slight, gives a catch or half breath that helps materially in keeping the singer supplied with air. Soloists are familiar with this technique and use it extensively.

Another simple and commonly used means of breath reinforcement is through so-called "individual," as contrasted to "group," breathing. By this method any singer may take short catch breaths at any time during the singing of a phrase, thereby keeping himself supplied without affecting the continuity of the ensemble tone. Thus, a group may sustain a chord indefinitely if it wills, without the audience being **made** aware of the mechanics which make the sustention possible. Inasmuch as singers vary in individual breath resources, this is a very practical bit of technique, provided the inhalations are so staggered that no two singers are breathing at exactly the same time. Only one more observation on breathing as an adjunct of phrasing seems necessary. This is that at rests or deliberate pauses in the music for effect or for group breath, the inhalation must be timed so as *not to retard the following attack*. Since there are just so many beats in a given measure, we cannot use additional time for breath without being short in our accounts at the end of the measure. Therefore, if a group breath is taken between contiguous notes, the *time for the breath should be taken from the note preceding it*. This practice permits the ensuing note to be attacked *on time*— a "must," if we are to maintain the pulse and tempo of the piece.

PHRASING FOR THE TEXT

Second, we should consider phrasing from the standpoint of rhetorical pause and we should conform to the outlines of the text. The composer naturally moulds his music so that the pauses, emphases, and dramatic climaxes of the text are preserved or enlarged. A thorough study of the text is therefore necessary as a prelude to forming a phrase pattern. Once made, this pattern should be *plainly marked on the music* and discussed in the rehearsal so that the singers may know exactly for what effects they are striving and so that exactness and uniformity may grow into the performance of them. The aimless, free-for-all, catch-as-catch-can phrasing of some amateur groups is execrable and is an affront to the language, the music, and the intelligence of singers and audience.

A. T. Davison has so aptly described the far too common insufficiency in this phase of performance that a quotation seems in order.

> Some choral conductors never avail themselves of the opportunity to illuminate the text, enhance the musical interest, and humanize the whole project by calling even for the phrasings that accompany ordinary conversation, to say nothing of the little lifts and pauses that stimulate. interest and add distinction to the singing. For them the only punctuation mark is the final period.
>
> Phrasing, aside from the categorical requirements set by punctuation, is a matter for the conductor's ingenuity. It is based on the principle of silence as effective contrast to sound. As choral conductors, we are far too indifferent to the validity of that principle, the prolonged moment which heightens expectation before the first note is heard; the momentary immobility of conductor and chorus which succeeds the final note and prevents the destruction of an impressive occasion by too prompt applause. But far more important are those constantly occurring situations when even the slightest interruption of the music is vital to its effectiveness.[7]

The matter of the value of rests in the music score, as a powerful element in interpretation, deserves full consideration by the director and offers him highly productive bypaths of exploration. We should not forget that rests are as definite a part of the music as are the notes, that they are placed where they are for a definite purpose. Too often the rests are relegated to the merely utilitarian status of serving as intervals for taking breath. Inhalation will occur during rests as a matter of course, but they should not be regarded as merely convenient filling stations along the musical highway. To achieve their designed purpose, they should be strictly observed for the total of their allotted time. This does not mean

[7] Davison, *op. cit.*, p. 68.

that they should be extended *beyond* it, unless for a deliberate purpose. Alteration of the notation either of notes or of rests is an assumption which only sober judgment should validate, and such alteration should be undertaken with full realization of the responsibility involved.

Rests, when properly observed, highlight both preceding phrases and those following, through the above-mentioned contrast between silence and sound; it seems foolish to strive for emphasis by putting on power when many times the emphasis is ready at hand through the observance of a well-timed rest. The deliberately interpolated pause, when aptly used, is one of the most potent effects in choral singing. It is like the poignant moment of suspense before the bursting of a tempest and gives what has preceded it—but particularly what follows—tremendous significance.

Again, in dramatic passages rests may be improvised between salient phrases or words, thus serving to set them out starkly like buttes in a desert plain. The employment of staccato may also be powerfully effective in lending emphasis to a phrase which might otherwise remain insignificant. Let the director treat the rest in choral music with the respect it deserves and find that like the ubiquitous popular drink, it is the "pause that refreshes."

To sum up the matter of phrasing, let us consider it our first duty to abide by the literary requirements of the text and the markings of the composer, whenever present; to utilize natural pauses for breath, thereby killing two musical birds with one stone; but never to fall so low in the scale of musicianship that we allow our units to breathe between syllables of a word or after pronouns, prepositions, verbs, or adverbs. Let us consider every phrase in its relation to the whole rather than in an isolated manner, and thus preserve the continuity of music and text. Let us contribute our fair share to *education through music* by encouraging integrity to cultural standards in the clothing of the outlines of our musical thought.

FUNDAMENTALS OF CHORAL EXPRESSION

DYNAMICS

Last, but by no means least, in our consideration of the problem of performance by choral groups, we come to the problem of dynamics—the varying degrees of power used in singing. Use of power should always be attended by a sense of responsibility and, in the adolescent choral field, as pointed out in the chapter on tone production, power and refined vocal quality are rarely wedded. If they are mated at all, they approach the marriage altar rather late in choral life.

Dynamics in youthful singing groups concern themselves much more with explorations of soft, rather than loud, gradations of the scale of tone volume. Does this mean that young singers are never to experience the thrill that comes from crescendo and the complete abandonment of self to a ringing climax? Certainly not! The fact that youth should not attempt to live the experiences that rightfully belong to later years does not rob them of the capacity for complete enjoyment of the life and things that are normally in their grasp. Just so, we must not expect that high-school choral groups should attempt to explore realms of dynamics which are reserved for the vocal maturity of adulthood. We have but to remember that dynamic markings in choral music are purely relative—to be interpreted in the light of contrast—and we shall find that a wide freedom and elasticity are still available to adolescents, even if we cannot consider the youthful choral ensemble as a powerhouse.

THE CIRCLE OF INTENSITY

It seems pertinent to describe the logical area of dynamics in any given choral unit as an imaginary circle, the circumference of which may represent the *maximum tone volume* which it can attain *without loss of quality* or of *complete ease of production*. All the area outside the circumference of this circle, therefore, is strictly taboo; and we should label the curving boundary of the circle "fortissimo," since the circle's circumference represents the ultimate in this group's propensity for power. The point at the center of the circle we may conceive as the unit's ultimate "pianissimo," or the *softest tone volume* which it can sing *without loss of quality and with complete ease.*

Immediately, then, we begin to sense the infinite number of gradations of power which are available to the ensemble in shading the tone volume to its needs. Varying ages and degrees of experience in singing will determine the circle of potentiality for each group, but whatever the individual circle dimension may be, the degrees of radiation from the tonal center will represent tremendous possibilities of dynamic expression.

With such a concept as the basis of his scale of volume, the director may go blithely about his business of performance with the confidence that at no time will he be under the necessity of sacrificing quality for quantity, nor be lacking in resources to adorn his product with the magic hues of light and shade.

THE SWELL

Much of the effectiveness of expression in choral music is inherent in the swell, which denotes both increase and diminution of volume; but like so many other effects in music, if it is not deftly handled, the swell may become a mechanical mannerism. Methodical repetition of wave-like undulations in tone is not artistic, nor does it connote the type of swell to be sought. Sir Arthur Sullivan once peremptorily stopped a Leeds festival chorus, which had been taught to indulge itself in that kind of mannerism, and said, "Please, let us have no more of that accordion expression."

Monotony of pattern anesthetizes musical emotion, and the swell, to be effective, must represent the rise and fall of poetic feeling. Pure emotion does not lend itself to delivery in uniform cartons, F.O.B.—the chorus; hence designs of shading should not be repeated with mathematical regularity. Swells

87

should be definite both in outline and in duration and should mirror the warmth of feeling which the particular phrase of the text and music suggests. Like an incoming tide, there may be mountainous billows that sweep in with foaming crests, followed by quiet undulations as gentle as a caress—the pattern endlessly changing. So with the swell in the choir. It may come as a sudden throb; a fulsome sigh; a slow, deepening surge that mounts gradually to an ecstasy, or a faint, final stir before the last note dies away. The possibilities of variation are endless, and the implications of poetic meaning unlimited.

THE STRAIGHT TONE

In contrast to the swell, the ensemble should be able to sustain tone for extended periods at any given dynamic within its radius of volume. Swells are effective only if they come from somewhere and so return; no director has the license to tinker with the delicate mechanism of the swell until his tonal engine can purr along indefinitely at a given intensity. The choir that can maintain this evenness of dynamic has a foundation for expression that is rock-ribbed. The emission of a pure, steady thread of tone has been a test of the singer's art since the days of Caccini. The late W. J. Henderson, dean of American music critics, described it as the basis for the *cantilena*, adding, "If you have no cantilena, you are no singer." [8] Unfortunately, too many directors do not make the *cantilena* precept number one in their approach to the problem of dynamics; they attempt to rear the ornamental façade before the foundation is in.

As to the size of the group's fundamental *cantilena*, we refer to the problem of tone production in suggesting that for young groups it be the soft, pure tone previously cited as a goal. Age and experience in its use will, of course, mature it, but it must not be so big that the swells from it transgress the circling boundary of the group's ultimate volume. Nor must the

[8] W. J. Henderson, *The Art of Singing*, New York: The Dial Press, 1938, p. 26.

cantilena always be soft. There are moments when sustained fullness is demanded, and when such moments come, the ensemble must be ready to meet the demand. Let the objective be to develop the ability to hold true and steady to the given degree of intensity suggested by music and text, and to move to and fro from a basic even tone into swells of whatever dimension emotion dictates and the radius of intensity permits. A further salutary effect of an even tone dynamic lies in its prevention of the common group habit consistently to diminish toward the ends of phrases. Such diminuendos are partly due to lack of breath supply (which can be avoided) and part is simply habit. Whatever the cause, it is a tonally anemic mannerism which may well be avoided.

Not all the dynamic effects applicable to a given piece will be found in the terminology occurring in the score. Such terms are safe guides to the composer's intent, and the conductor should have so accurate a knowledge of their meaning that he can faithfully carry out the suggested design; but many of the effects may occur as the result of the emotional sensitivity of the director, which, if it be refined and truly poetic, is strongly to be encouraged.

PARTIAL EMPHASIS

Finally, the use of dynamics in ensemble embraces more than the simultaneous use of patterns by all voice sections. Evenness of tone does not imply that various voice parts are to be equally intense at all times. On chords it may be necessary to subdue or increase certain tones in the interest of balance. Since the days of the experiments of Pythagoras we have known that the third is a strong influence in the key tonality. Moving parts and altered tones, or notes of modulation or resolution, need momentary eminence, and the director must be ever vigilant to the possibility and need of such occasions.

The elevation of an inner voice may create an interval of charm that is eloquent and, in contrapuntal passages, the entrance of a theme will certainly call for stress. Whenever a melody is present in any voice, balance becomes unbalance in the sense that the melody must have predominance over subordinate parts. The predominance is much better attained by reducing the accompanying voices rather than by straining the melody voice to sing above the others.

At times one is forced to listen to a modest small school group attempting to sing some misguided arrangement of a waltz, such as the "Blue Danube." The piece usually has an unvaried pattern of "Lah-lah's" on after beats in the lower voices—all of which sing as loud as, if not louder than, the section carrying the melody. In both tone quality and effect, the ensemble resembles nothing so much as a village band playing some perennial "Um, pah-pah" number, during which the "pahs" get the better of the "ums" most of the time.

Such a dynamic monstrosity is a violation not only of balance but also of rhythmic accent which demands that strong beats of the measure be stressed according to need and that weak beats be subordinated.

There are instances when vivid dynamic accent forms practically the whole design for expression. When this occurs, the effect is best achieved by the sudden hushing of subordinate beats, leaving the strong accents free to maintain a stirring virile pattern, unhampered by over-intrusion of the others. Few errors are more deadly than the monotonous, even accent on all measure beats sometimes heard in amateur groups. This equal stress on all beats actually results in no accent at all, and whatever vitality may have been inherent in the music withers and dies before the first period is sung.

In summarizing the suggestions for dealing with the problems of dynamics, let us, as directors, learn the correct dimensions of our groups' *circles of intensity* and stay *within them.* Let us lay a foundation of even, pure tonal intensity on which to base the swell—the peak of choral expression. Let us be sensitive to balance, which inheres in both group unanimity and in partial emphasis. Let us sing melody pre-eminently whenever it occurs, for melody is created to be thematic, individual, and distinct; and let us conform to natural laws of accent and rhythm which are vested in contrast. Above all, let us consider that, in controlled dynamics, we have a wide freedom in the use of materials with which to build citadels of spiritual beauty.

Epilogue

》》》➤≪≪

*. . . And there was taken up
of fragments that remained
to them twelve baskets.—St.
Luke IX:17.*

》》》➤≪≪

THE cook, the seamstress, and the carpenter always have fragments that remain. Indeed, in any work there is always some residue of elements used in the making of the original. Remnants are not always waste and much of value may be inherent in them.

At the end of the study the writer finds many details occurring to him which he wishes might have been included in the body of the text, but he is reconciled to the inevitability of residue and hence contents himself by appending twelve small baskets of "materia musica" which dropped by the wayside during the investigation. They are culled from the many details which help to achieve choral craftsmanship, and though perhaps not of indispensable nature, they may contribute their quota to artistic group musical expression.

1. Use care in the selection of an accompanist. Choral accompanying is excellent training for any student, but musicianship in the accompaniment is vital; if inadequacy is present in that phase of the work, the effect on the chorus is bound to be disintegrating and costly. Therefore, strive to secure a quality of accompanying which will, in itself, constitute both support and leadership.

It is good stagecraft not to conduct the piano preludes or interludes. Have prearranged, unobtrusive signals for beginning, and let the chorus and director give an impression of listening to the prelude—just as the soloist does—waiting with anticipation for the moment of attack. Do not organize automatic rests at the end of the prelude. Begin *on time* by establishing a feeling of definite rhythm which starts at the first note of the accompaniment and continues until the piece is finished. Clean attacks and releases are vital to expressiveness.

2. Train the ensemble from the first rehearsal to watch the director. When music is used, the singers should hold it high enough to see the conductor easily over its top. Teach the group the habit of looking at the director at least on every second measure. This procedure encourages concentration both on the score and on the direction. The eyes should rest easily on the conductor in an expression of eager anticipation. From the moment the director takes his conducting position, he—and he only—should be the center of attention until the number ends.

3. In rehearsing repertoire, beware of stopping the chorus too frequently even though errors are present. New material should be sung or scanned throughout at proper tempo, regardless of inaccuracies, in order to give the ensemble a general concept of the style and spirit of the piece; singers may hum, sing, or remain silent during the first playing of the number. While pieces are "in work," concentrate on one element of rendition at a time, giving instructions at the start and then allowing the chorus to sing until it reaches a prearranged stopping place. If single passages need attention, practice them as definite units, but avoid habitual interruptions which waste time and create exasperation in singers. Follow the sound educational principle of working from *whole* to *part*.

4. Oral reading of the score helps to fix rhythmic outlines in the minds of singers and also helps to secure distinctness in consonants. In numbers that have rapid tempos, voices are spared, valuable time is saved, and clear-cut patterns of rendition are often secured by this simple device.

5. In performance avoid counterfeit emotion and cheap sentimentalism, which violate every tenet of musicianship.[1]

[1] Dann, "Some Essentials of Choral Singing," Music Educators National Conference, 1932.

Cold, unemotional singing, devoid of feeling, is better than crass sentimentalism. "Crooning," slurring, and cheap effects borrowed from popular radio programs are beyond the pale of choral musicianship. One of the most obnoxious of these effects is the mannered closing of final *m's* and *n's* into a hum. No sensitive director will permit the growth of such ill-favored choral etiquette in his groups.

6. Foster an ever-developing spirit of attention at rehearsals. Some groups form the habit of talking like a bevy of magpies the moment a musical passage or composition is completed. They do this, not with the intent to be discourteous to the director, but through lack of training in habits of attention. No discipline should be enforced which inhibits a complete sense of freedom in the membership, but promiscuous talking can utterly ruin the atmosphere and the objectives of any rehearsal. The practice period should be a concisely directed interval of song rather than a choral Kaffeeklatsch. Let there be frequent moments of relaxation, but from the very beginning let the director secure the cooperation of the membership in developing habits of attention which will make all working intervals in the rehearsal inviolable. Cultivate the habit of complete silence on the part of the group after any period of musical activity until the director has commented upon it. Such a habit induces curiosity as to what he *may* say and helps singers to strive for approval; it also puts the director on his mettle to make his comments of either praise or criticism worth waiting for.

On the other hand, let the conductor himself learn to refrain from talking overmuch. It is much better to *sing* offending passages than to "talk them to death." Imitation of group errors in diction, if neatly done, may correct a fault almost instantly. The mimicry should be deft, whimsical, without sting; if it calls for a laugh, let it be enjoyed by all. For instance, if the unit insists on singing the words "and the night" as if it were "an-nuh-night," the director may stop the chorus abruptly by saying, "Anna Knight! Who is she?" and the error may not occur again. Talking to the group while it is actually singing is a valuable bit of form when it is well done. To be constructive in this, however, the director must constantly be a step ahead of the singers; by means of a terse direction as to diction, emphasis, or dynamic, *just preceding the moment of utterance,* he may guide the ensemble to the desired end. For instance, a quick "What?" or "Who?" from the conductor in advance of a word or phrase he wants stressed, may elicit an emphatic answer in the music from the singers that will give just the effect desired.

7. In performance, the stage pattern and the poise of a group have a strong bearing upon its effectiveness. If a stage curtain is part of the equipment, let the choir be in place before the curtain is opened. In the absence of a curtain, the group should take its position with precision and alacrity, walking briskly in well-planned formation. Two lines entering from opposite sides of the stage are better than one seemingly interminable queue. Avoid all mannerisms of position, such as the abrupt folding of the hands at a given signal. Let the singers take the desired hand position naturally and unobtrusively as each arrives at his appointed place. All erratic mannerisms are out of rapport with the spirit of art. No mechanics should be allowed to levy a toll upon the business of *interpreting the music,* which is the singers' first, last, and only duty.

In festivals and contests, some directors seem never satisfied with the position of their groups; they seem obliged to maneuver the ensemble, collectively or individually, to right or left—or both—using the motions of a parking-lot official. This is an abuse of the waiting audience and can be avoided by careful planning in advance.

8. Strive to encourage an animated facial expression in every singer. True, some music is serious; some is even sad, but there is sentiment still, and faces must be alive to mirror it. When units sing gay, light-hearted music with stolid, impassive mien—not unlike Grant Wood's study in American Gothic—

one is moved to wonder whether, after all, singing is an act from which all joy has fled. Some groups seem automatically to assume a stoic immobility of expression the moment the music starts, never to regain the vivid animation of youth until the danger of using it in the song has passed. Such practice is the direct and absolute reverse of the ideal concept; from the first rehearsal singers should be urged to allow their facial expressions complete freedom in mirroring the mood of the text. This does not mean that an artificial, tailored grin should characterize the singing, for that may be as unnatural as a frozen dullness. The secret of facial expression in singing dwells in the *eyes*. *Keep the eyes alight and full of the meaning of the text.* The remaining elements in the gamut of facial expression will naturally follow.

9. In building program repertoire, see that the element of contrast is duly observed. Even good music palls when it is of unvaried pattern. Moods of nature and men are forever on the wing; it is to the variety of man's moods that we owe the vast, varied repertoire which is the singer's heritage. Pieces of the same general period should be grouped together, but these also should be varied within their separate groupings. Never alternate sacred and humorous numbers. Striking contrast should occur between groups of pieces rather than within them.[2] Strongly effective pieces should be chosen for beginning and ending the program. It is always well to have some number tucked away that *everybody will enjoy;* this is good program making. Arrange the continuity of a joint group program to achieve climax of interest and effectiveness. Remember that in music, also, variety is the spice of life.

10. If possible, organize group voice classes as an adjunct to the specialized choral group program; they are a powerful aid in developing talent which will be invaluable in ensembles. The same basic tone production technique used for ensembles should also be used in such voice classes, where the instructor

[2] Christy, *op. cit.*, p. 87.

has an ample opportunity to develop it. The two types of activity work admirably together.

11. Do not delay public appearance of various groups too long. Let the experience in performance parallel the development of the ensembles. This statement does not mean that the innocent public should be made to listen to *half-readied* units. It does mean that as certain pieces attain finish, the director should accept available opportunities for group performances. Waiting until an over-zealous director feels that perfection is achieved may invite a sense of defeatism and inferiority in the groups. When at last they do appear under such a philosophy, the results may be so unsatisfactory as to dull the thrist for expression. Units should be given opportunity as frequently as their development permits to crystallize their training habits by performing before an audience. The growth in valid applied expression is strongly actuated thereby.

12. Strive to build a true democracy in every ensemble. This connotes a mutual spirit of "all for one and one for all." A sense of superiority has no place in the choral group. Music belongs to everybody, and the unattainable heights to which it ever beckons should keep its devoted followers sufficiently humble to restrain them from any feeling of eminence, which some momentary local achievement may bring. No matter how talented we may be, someone else is just a step ahead. Membership in groups should not constitute an elevated social rating. Rather it should merely increase the capacity of the student for service in the workshop of art.

The onus for any or all of the problems which have engaged our attention in this study rests inevitably with the director; for it is he, and he only, who must sense them and provide the solution. His is a challenging responsibility which calls for multiple high qualities if the music which he unfolds to his singers is to be the moving force in education and life which is within its province.

He must be first of all a teacher in the full sense of the word, a mentor, following the pattern of his legendary forebear who accepted the responsibility for the education of the son of his absent friend—Odysseus. Thus he must be versed in sound educational procedure; he must be able to offer guidance for problems of life, as well as of music, out of mutual student-teacher experiences which are highly potent for guidance; most of all, he must have the ability and erudition to open up for those who are entrusted to his charge fascinating fields of mental and spiritual adventure. Such "a teacher," said Henry B. Adams, "affects eternity; he can never tell where his influence stops."

Again, the director must possess instincts of refinement and culture. No one should assume to lead student excursions into the spiritual, emotional, and imaginative fields of art who has not, within himself, the enlightenment and vision to point out compelling beauties wherever they may be found.

Lastly, the director must have an authentic musicianship, a broad knowledge of the field he serves, and a fidelity to its standards and cause which admits of no compromise. He must be able to recognize worthy instincts of expression, no matter how humble their origin; when they are not evident, he must seek means to stir them into being and then with zest guide and mould them into eloquence of beauty. In such fascinating enterprise he may have the thrilling conviction that he too works with eternal verities for "there is no truer truth obtainable by man than comes of music."

RECOMMENDED READING

BOOKS

BILLETT, R. O., *Fundamentals of Secondary School Teaching,* New York: Houghton Mifflin Company, 1940.

BODEGRAVEN, PAUL VAN, AND WILSON, HARRY R., *The School Music Conductor,* Chicago: Hall & McCreary, 1942.

CAIN, NOBLE, *Choral Music and Its Practice,* New York: Witmark & Sons, 1932.

CHRISTY, VAN A., *Glee Club and Chorus,* New York: G. Schirmer, 1940.

COWARD, HENRY, *Choral Technique and Interpretation,* London: Novello and Co.; H. W. Gray Co., New York, sole agents for the U. S. A.

DANN, HOLLIS, *Conductor's Book,* New York: American Book Co., 1936.

DAVISON, A. T., *Choral Conducting,* Cambridge: Harvard University Press, 1940.

DAVISON, A. T., *Music Education in America,* New York: Harper & Bros., 1926.

DYKEMA, PETER W., AND GEHRKENS, KARL E., *High School Music,* Boston: C. C. Birchard, 1941.

FINN, WM. J., *The Art of the Choral Conductor,* Boston: C. C. Birchard & Co., 1939.

GREENE, H. P., *Interpretation in Song,* London: Macmillan & Co., 1934.

HENDERSON, W. J., *The Art of Singing,* New York: Dial Press, 1938.

MURSELL, JAMES L., *Human Values in Music Education,* New York: Silver Burdette and Company, 1934.

MURSELL, JAMES L., *Music in American Schools,* Boston: Silver Burdette and Company, 1943.

MURSELL, JAMES L., AND GLENN, MABELLE, *Psychology of School Music Teaching,* Boston: Silver Burdette and Company, 1938.

PITTS, CAROL, *Voice Class Method,* Chicago: Kjos, 1936.

ROGERS, CLARA K., *Your Voice and You,* Boston: Oliver Ditson, 1925.

SMALLMAN, JOHN, AND WILCOX, JOHN C., *The Art of A Cappella Singing,* Boston: Oliver Ditson, 1933.

STARCH, DANIEL, STANTON, HASEL M., AND KOERTH WILHELMINE, *Psychology of Education,* New York: Appleton-Century, 1941.

SHAKESPEARE, WILLIAM, *The Art of Singing,* Boston: Oliver Ditson, 1910.

WITHERSPOON, HERBERT, *Singing,* New York: G. Schirmer, 1925.

ZANZIG, A. D., *Music in American Life,* New York: Oxford University Press, 1932.

\Y, HENRI, *Psychology of Voice and of Life,* New York: G. Schirmer, 1917.

FUNDAMENTALS OF CHORAL EXPRESSION

ARTICLES

BACH, IDA E., "Training the A Cappella Choir," Yearbook, Music Educators National Conference, 1935.

BOETTE, MARIA, "Training the A Cappella Choir," Yearbook, Music Educators National Conference, 1935.

BRENNAN, R. E., "The Gregorian Tradition in the History of Music," Yearbook, Music Educators National Conference, 1939–40.

BURUS, S. T., "Problems of the Choral Conductor in Small High Schools," Yearbook, Music Educators National Conference, 1932.

CAIN, NOBLE, "Choral Fads and Jitterbug Fancies," Yearbook, Music Educators National Conference, 1939–40.

CHRISTIANSON, F. M., "Ensemble Singing," Yearbook, Music Educators National Conference, 1932.

DANN, HOLLIS, "Some Essentials of Choral Singing," Yearbook, Music Educators National Conference, 1937.

EVANSON, J. A., "Classroom Choral Technique," Yearbook, Music Educators National Conference, 1932.

EVANSON, J. A., "Pieces or Fundamentals," Music Educators Journal, Vol. XVI, No. 2 (Oct., 1936).

GLENN, MABELLE, "A New Goal in Ensemble Singing," Music Educators Journal, Vol. XV, No. 2 (Oct., 1928).

HANSON, HOWARD, "Music in American Life," Yearbook, Music Educators National Conference, 1939.

HOWERTON, GEORGE, "Music Education through Choral Experience," Yearbook, Music Educators National Conference, 1939.

HUBBARD, G. E., "Some Notes on Conducting," Music Educators Journal, Vol. XXII (May, 1936).

KRONE, MAX T., AND WALLACE, FLORENCE M., "High School Students' Interest in Choral Music," Music Educators Journal, Vol. XXI, No. 2 (Oct., 1934).

LANSBURY, J. L., "Education through Music," Yearbook, Music Educators National Conference, 1939.

MORGAN, R. V., "Analyzing Objectives in Music Education," Bulletin of the Department of Secondary School Principals of the National Education Association, No. 45 (March, 1933).

OSBORNE, R. L., "Ensemble Singing in the Senior High School," Music Educators Journal, Vol. XVI, No. 2 (Dec., 1929).

PITTS, CAROL, "Securing Correct Intonation in the Training of A Cappella Choirs," Yearbook, Music Educators National Conference, 1932.

SPOUSE, ALFRED, "Report of Master Vocal Class Conducted," Yearbook, Music Educators National Conference, 1939.

VELD, HENRY, "Choral Conducting," Proceedings, Music Teachers National Association, 1934.

VELD, HENRY, "Some Practical Thoughts on Choral Singing," Proceedings, Music Teachers National Association, 1936.

RECOMMENDED READING

WAGNER, A. H., "Research in the Field of Voice Training," Yearbook, Music Educators National Conference, 1939.

WILHOUSKY, PETER J., "Choral Conducting," Yearbook, Music Educators National Conference, 1937.

YOUNG, J. C., "Vocal Diction in a Nut Shell," Music Educators Journal, Vol. XIX, No. 1 (Oct., 1932).